THE LAW OF
MUSICAL AND DRAMATIC COPYRIGHT.

BY

EDWARD CUTLER,
ONE OF HER MAJESTY'S COUNSEL,

THOMAS EUSTACE SMITH AND
FREDERIC E. WEATHERLY,
ESQUIRES, BARRISTERS-AT-LAW.

REVISED EDITION.

CASSELL & COMPANY, LIMITED:
LONDON, PARIS & MELBOURNE.
1892.
[ALL RIGHTS RESERVED.]

CONTENTS.

	PAGE
INTRODUCTION	1—9
DRAMATIC COPYRIGHT	10—26
GENERAL REMARKS	10
NATURE, EXTENT, AND DURATION OF THE RIGHT	10
WHO IS AN AUTHOR?	12
DRAMATISATION OF NOVELS AND OTHER WORKS	14
WHAT IS A DRAMATIC COMPOSITION?	18
WHAT IS A PLACE OF DRAMATIC ENTERTAINMENT?	19
HOW THE RIGHT OF REPRESENTATION IS TRANSFERRED	22
INFRINGEMENT AND REMEDY	22
WHAT IS CONSENT WITHIN THE ACT?	23
WHO IS AN OFFENDER WITHIN THE ACT?	24
THE NATURE OF THE SUM RECOVERABLE BY THE INJURED PARTY	25
LIMITATION OF ACTION	26
MUSICAL AND DRAMATIC COPYRIGHT	27—71
GENERAL REMARKS	27
WHO MAY POSSESS COPYRIGHT?	28
IN WHAT COPYRIGHT MAY EXIST	30
DURATION OF COPYRIGHT PROPER	35
DURATION OF PERFORMING RIGHTS	36
DURATION OF COPYRIGHT IN THE CASE OF PERIODICALS	37
TRANSFER OF COPYRIGHT	39
REGISTRATION AT STATIONERS' HALL	47
JUDICIAL DEFINITION OF PROPRIETOR	47
NAME OF PUBLISHER	54
PLACE OF PUBLICATION	54
PERIODICALS	54
EDITIONS	54
DELIVERY OF COPIES AT BRITISH MUSEUM, ETC.	55
INFRINGEMENT OF RIGHTS	57
INFRINGEMENT OF COPYRIGHT PROPER	57

MUSICAL AND DRAMATIC COPYRIGHT (continued):—
- INFRINGEMENT OF PERFORMING RIGHTS 60
- LITERARY LARCENY 64
- REMEDIES FOR INFRINGEMENT 68
- REMEDY FOR PIRACY BY ACTION ON THE CASE . . 68
- SPECIAL PENALTY FOR UNLAWFUL IMPORTATION . . 69
- REMEDY BY INJUNCTION 71

INTERNATIONAL COPYRIGHT 72
- INTRODUCTORY REMARKS 72
- TREATIES WITH FOREIGN COUNTRIES 73
- THE BERNE CONVENTION 74
- THE RETROSPECTIVE OPERATION OF RECENT ENACT-
  MENTS . . . . 81—86
- WHAT AMOUNTS TO PUBLICATION 87
- TRANSLATIONS OF WORKS THE SUBJECT OF INTERNATIONAL
  COPYRIGHT 91
- EXTENSION OF INTERNATIONAL COPYRIGHT TO COLONIES 98
- THE LAW OF COPYRIGHT BETWEEN GREAT BRITAIN AND
  THE COLONIES 105
- CANADIAN COPYRIGHT 106

APPENDIX 115
- THE INTERNATIONAL COPYRIGHT ACT, 1886 . . . 115

APPENDIX II. 127
- ORDER-IN-COUNCIL OF THE 28TH NOVEMBER, 1887 . 127
- THE BERNE CONVENTION 130

APPENDIX III. 146
- FORMS OF AGREEMENT, ETC., ON SALES, ETC., OF COPYRIGHT 146
- NOTE AS TO LIABILITY TO ROYALTY PASSING TO SUB-
  PURCHASER 153

APPENDIX IV.—RECENT ALTERATIONS IN LAW OF UNITED STATES 154
APPENDIX V.—TEXT OF THE AMERICAN STATUTE OF 1891 . . 159
APPENDIX VI—NECESSITY FOR REGISTRATION BY FOREIGNER
  SUING HERE 162
APPENDIX VII.—TERMS OF FOREIGN COPYRIGHT . . . 164
INDEX 165
ABBREVIATIONS 171
CASE INDEX 173

MUSICAL AND DRAMATIC COPYRIGHT.

INTRODUCTION.

THE axiom that a little knowledge is a dangerous thing applies, it must be admitted, in all its force to litigation. Law has been described as a razor of preternatural sharpness, more remarkable for shaving very close than for always shaving the right man; and even if some of us, actuated by a sentimental attachment to our profession, deny the general application of this description, few will doubt its correctness when the weapon is wielded by inexperienced hands. The law of copyright is, however, an exception to this rule; the legal and literary professions readily assimilate; the abstract reasoning power necessary for success in the one has to be cultivated in a diluted form by the disciples of the other; and cases often occur, like that of the late Mr. Charles Reade, where amateurs have successfully argued in person cases in which they have been interested; and not only have kept clear of the stigma attached by popular opinion to the client of the man who is his own lawyer, but have held their own against eminent professional advocates. Cheered by this reflection the writers have aimed at combining in this little work matter appealing to two classes; they hope to have attained precision enough to satisfy the requirements of professional lawyers; and on the

Reade v. Bentley, 4 K. & J. 656.

other hand to be of use to litigants, actual or in contemplation, who, though prevented by modesty from arguing a question on the rule in Shelley's case, may consider that their legal knowledge justifies them in pleading in person for the exclusive right to represent a scene in a pantomime, or to multiply copies of a song.

It would be going beyond the limits of this work to trace in detail the development of the law of copyright from its origin in the seventeenth century; whereas our book is only intended to deal with more recent subject-matter, viz.: the rights of dramatic authors and composers, home and international. Those rights are defined by a series of enactments commencing with a statute of William the Fourth, passed in the year 1833. But as questions turning on the law of musical and dramatic copyright will be more readily understood by persons who have some acquaintance with the previous law, a short account of that law is given in this Introduction.

It may for the purpose of the lay reader be necessary to explain that it was in the first instance not alone under Copyright Acts that an author could claim protection for his works.

Prior to any statute the common law protected an author in the enjoyment of his work, but this common law or inherent right has now almost passed from the region of practice into that of history, as the modern statutes regulate the majority of conceivable cases. This form of literary property prior to and outside legislative enactment is, however, recognised and shown by the language of a statute passed as early as 1662, in a clause prohibiting the public from printing without the consent of the owner a book which any person had the sole right to print under Letters Patent, or by virtue of any entry in the Register Book of the Company of Stationers, or in the Register Book of either of the Universities.

13 & 14 Car. II., c. 33.

Copinger. 2nd Ed., p. 22.

The often-cited " Statute of Anne " enacted in effect that authors of books not then printed should have the sole right of printing for fourteen years and no longer. A penalty was laid on any person publishing, importing, or selling piratical copies; and a registration clause was added for purposes of publicity; which latter clause has formed the foundation for the numerous registration provisos inserted in subsequent Acts. The clause in question enacted that no book was to be entitled to protection unless the title had been entered before publication in the Register Book of the Stationers' Company; that nine copies of each book should be delivered to the warehouse keeper of the said Company for the use of the Royal Library in London, the Universities, Sion College, and the Library of the Faculty for Edinburgh, under a penalty. A clause was also inserted in the Act of Anne, which has been found useful in modern legislation, prohibiting importation without the written consent of the owner. After the expiration of the term of fourteen years the sole right of printing or disposing of copies was to return to the authors, if living, for another term of fourteen years.

_{8 Anne, c. 19.}

This statute was held in the case of Donaldson v. Becket (which stands out as a conspicuous landmark in the history of copyright) to have extinguished by implication the natural or inherent right of property in an author's work; and to cut him down to the right, if any, which he might have by positive enactment.

<sub>4 Burr. 2408
2 Bro. Parl.
Cas. 129.</sub>

The Statute of Anne has been long since repealed.

It may be useful to point out to the lay reader what may not be self-evident, viz.: that it is a very different matter whether a claim be laid under the common law, or by virtue of a statute. In the first case the right would be a perpetual one; whereas an Act of Parliament, while it gives the author the benefit of a statutory remedy, cuts down the duration of that right to a limited time; and in this respect the author is treated with less, and the public with more, liberality under English law than in many European States. The longest period of copyright known to our law is the natural life of the author and a further term of seven years, or an absolute period of forty-two years; whereas the duration under French law is the term of fifty years from the death of the author, in which respect the example of our neighbours is followed by those European States in which the Code Napoléon, or an adaptation of it, prevails. Again, those who claim under the statute are subject to rigorous enactments enforcing registration.

The importance of the distinction between a right by virtue of, and one outside legislative enactment, is shown by the fact that in one case the struggle to escape from the effect of a statutory clause providing that no author should have copyright outside the Act containing the clause, created considerable litigation. Mr. Boucicault, having for the first time published an original play, *The Colleen Bawn*, in New York, sought to restrain an English infringer. The defenant showed that the plaintiff could not rely on any statute; the policy of our Legislature being to protect only those works which are first published in Great Britain, or in a country with which this country has a treaty; whereas there was no treaty with the United States. Had it not been for the clause referred to, Mr. Boucicault might have said, "I do not want your statutes, I claim none of the specific remedies conferred by them, and I am not concerned to comply with their vexatious formalities. I take my stand on the common law of England, which entitles me to prosecute a marauder."

7 & 8 Vict., c. 12, s. 19.

Boucicault v. Delafield, 1 H. & M. 597.

It was held, however, that the clause in question applied literally, and that the plaintiff must come under statute or not at all.

The period of copyright was enlarged to twenty-eight years from publication, or the life of the author, whichever should be the longest, by a subsequent Act since repealed. 54 Geo. III., c. 156, s. 4.

This being the state of the law as regards literary copyright, it was not considered to be free from question whether a musical composition stood on the same footing as a book; but the affirmative was held after some discussion, and a sheet of music was also held to come within the definition of a "book" within the meaning of the Copyright Acts.

By an Act of King William the Fourth, the sole liberty of representing unpublished dramatic pieces was conferred upon the author or his assignee; the Act extended to the whole of the British Dominions, and the author of published dramatic pieces was to be entitled until twenty-eight years from publication, or if he should be then living, during the residue of his natural life, to the sole liberty of representing such pieces, and penalties were imposed upon infringers. Somewhat analogous provisions were contained in the Copyright Amendment Act, and the remedies for infringement of property in dramatic pieces were extended. Copyright in every book to be published in the life-time of the author after the passing of the Act was conferred upon such author for the period now existing, viz.: for seven years from his death, or the period of forty-two years, whichever should be the longest. As to books published after the death of the author, copyright was conferred for an absolute period of forty-two years. It is unnecessary for the purposes of this Introduction to refer to the stringent provisions contained in the Act with reference to registration and delivery of copies. It is important to note that all the provisions of the Act of William the Fourth were reserved to dramatic authors.

3 & 4 Will. IV., c. 15.

5 & 6 Vict., c. 45.

These statutes have substantially superseded all questions as to common law or inherent copyright in musical and dramatic pieces, and regulate the rights of authors of such pieces so far as regards the United Kingdom. In the year 1844 it was found necessary for meeting the exigencies of the period to adjust the international rights and liabilities of countries with which Great Britain was frequently brought into contact, and the ground was laid out and prepared for treaties dealing with the subject-matter. The machinery by which this desirable result was to be attained was as follows:—Legislative enactments empowering the Queen by Order in Council to confer copyright in England upon foreign authors or composers during the same period to which authors of similar works first published in the United Kingdom would have been entitled. These provisions extend to the sole liberty of representing dramatic pieces and musical compositions, as well as to the right of multiplying copies of such works. Provisions as to registration were inserted in the Act.

By a subsequent Act passed in the year 1852, a similar power was given to Her Majesty with reference to the translation of books emanating from foreign authors; an Order in Council might be levelled at the publication in the British Dominions of such translations, or against the representation thereof. By a somewhat obscure provision however, fair adaptations to the English stage of foreign dramatic works were excepted from the operation of the Act, and registration was made necessary.

The power so conferred on Her Majesty was exercised in the first instance by a Convention authorised by an Order in Council under the authority of the last-mentioned Act; by such Convention British and Prussian subjects had conferred upon them reciprocal rights with regard to works published in either of the countries parties to the treaty; the effect being that, on compliance with certain provisions as to registration, an author publishing a work in Prussia would be entitled to the same rights in England as an Englishman. Public representation or performance was put upon the same footing as copyright.

The example thus given was followed by all the other States which have since been consolidated in the German Empire; France followed suit in 1851; the Hanse Towns and Belgium were not far behind, and Spain and Sardinia concluded the list, the date of the treaty with the latter country being as recent as the year 1860.

With characteristic sagacity the United States of America kept aloof from the literary federation formed by these Conventions, and have reaped a rich harvest by their judicious abstention. It will be hereafter seen what large benefits have accrued to the American publishers by playing into the hands of Canada, and practically nullifying the provisions of the English International Copyright Acts as regards that dependency of Great Britain.

Many inconveniences have both theoretically and practically resulted from the relations created between this country and the other federated countries; there was no uniformity in the terms of the treaties, which varied in some material respects, notably in the matter of registration. For instance, in the case of the French Convention of 1851, registration in England within three months after the first publication of a work in France was a condition precedent to the existence of British copyright; and *vice versâ* the smallest deviation from the registration forms was held to invalidate the entry in the register; enormous sums have, owing to an omission by some ministerial agent to fulfil a minute technicality, been lost to men of genius who have been compelled to stand by and see their works pass, as it was then thought irrevocably, into the public domain. It is notorious that such was the case with reference to Gounod's opera of *Faust*.

The alleged necessity for some retroactive clauses to repair these evils, as well as the advantages which would obviously result from consolidating in one the treaties existing between the federated countries, were duly taken into consideration, with the result that a scheme was formed for confederating those countries with the addition of some others into one whole for the purposes of international copyright. This was accomplished in the year 1886 by a combination of the States which had formerly entered into treaties with Great Britain, with the addition of Haiti, Switzerland, and Tunis. The actual machinery is described in the body of this work; in popular language the general effect of the Union is—

(A) To protect unpublished works of any subject of any State a party to the Union.

(B) To protect works by an author of any nationality, if first published in any one of the federated States. Works published outside the federated States are unprotected, whatever the nationality of the author.

The rights conferred are in each country those which that country allows to its own subjects.

Thus for almost all purposes of copyright the federated countries are converted into one large domain, of which the inhabitants may sue one another, and be sued, without distinction of nationality. The exceptions to this character of literary kinship are to be found in that clause of the Convention which regulates the term of copyright, and the formalities necessary for entitling an author to its benefits. The period is not to be the same whether the work to be protected was first published in, for instance, Italy or England, but will vary according to locality, and the registration formalities are in like manner distributive and not homogeneous.

The clauses dealing with the retrospective effect of the

Convention, combined with an Act of Parliament which was passed to facilitate the great international change, have possibly sown the seed for considerable litigation. <small>49 & 50 Vict., c. 33.</small>

The document embodying the Convention is, however, in most respects framed with such clearness as to command the admiration of all lawyers, and the welcome of all disinterested ones.

CHAPTER I.

DRAMATIC COPYRIGHT.

General Remarks—The Nature, Extent, and Duration of Dramatic Copyright—Who is an Author?—How Copyright is Transferred—What is a Dramatic Composition?—What is a Place of Dramatic Entertainment?—Infringement—What is Consent?—Who is an "Offender" within the Dramatic Copyright Act?—Nature of the Remedy for Infringement—Limitation of Action.

GENERAL REMARKS.

THE author or owner of any literary composition or work of art has, while he keeps it unpublished, an absolute right to it at common law, and has the same remedies for wrongful appropriation and user as in the case of other chattels.

<small>Jeffreys v. Boosey, 4 H.L.C. 846.</small>

<small>Prince Albert v. Strange, 1 Mac. & Gor. 25.</small>

But directly he publishes, this common law right to exclude other persons is lost; and such rights as he then possesses are the express creations of statute.

Unless, therefore, he conforms to the various statutory conditions, he has no such rights, or at least he has no means of enforcing them.

Our considerations being limited to rights in dramatic and musical compositions, we may proceed at once to discuss the two statutes by virtue of which such rights are created, and may be enforced; considering in separate paragraphs the points which the various sections raise.

NATURE, EXTENT, AND DURATION OF THE RIGHT.

In section 1 of the Dramatic Copyright Act, it is enacted that "the author of any unprinted and unpublished dramatic piece, or the assignee of such author, shall have the sole liberty of representing or causing

<small>3 & 4 Wm. IV., c.15, s.1.</small>

to be represented at any place or places of dramatic entertainment whatsoever in any part of the British Dominions any such production as aforesaid, and shall be taken to be the proprietor thereof; and that the author of any such production printed and published within ten years before the passing of the Act, by the author thereof or his assignee, or which shall hereafter be so printed and published, or the assignee of such author, shall respectively until the end of twenty-eight years from the day of such first publication of the same, and also if the author or authors or survivor of the authors shall be living at the end of that period during the residue of his natural life, have as his own property the sole liberty of representing or causing to be represented the same at any such place of dramatic entertainment as aforesaid, and shall be taken to be the proprietor thereof."

Prior to this enactment, "the author of a dramatic (and musical) composition acquired under other statutes a copyright in his work only so far that he could prevent other persons from multiplying copies of it"—that is to say, he had copyright in his composition considered as a "book," but he had no right to control the representation. *Per* North, J., *in* Chappell *v.* Boosey, 21 Ch.D. 232.

This right of controlling the representation is created by the section above quoted, and it marks an important epoch in the history of dramatic literature. 3 & 4 Wm. IV., c.15, s. 1.

It will be observed that a difference is made between unpublished and published works. In the case of the former the duration of the right is not defined, while in the latter it is limited to twenty-eight years from the day of first publication, or for the natural life of the author or his assignee, whichever period be the longer.

The Copyright Amendment Act professes to "extend" the duration of these performing rights. This it does in terms in the case of printed and 5 & 6 Vict., c. 45, s. 4.

published dramatic works, the change being from twenty-eight years to forty-two, or the natural life of the proprietor, and seven years beyond, whichever period be the longer.

But the performing rights of dramatic works not printed and published being undefined by the Dramatic Copyright Act, the use of the term "extend" is confusing, and we are left in doubt whether the performing rights of such works last for the time specified by the Copyright Amendment Act, or for ever.

<small>3 & 4 Wm. IV., c. 15.</small>

WHO IS AN AUTHOR?

A definition will be found in Attwill v. Ferrett: "one who by his own intellectual labour applied to the materials of his composition produces an arrangement or compilation new in itself." Thus if A by his own intellectual labour writes a play, whether it is based on the facts of history or on the facts of A's experience, or on his imagination, or even on B's novel, A is the "author," and however hard it may appear to B that his novel should be the backbone of A's work, he cannot restrain the performance of the play so made; though he may prevent the multiplication of copies if they contain considerable and verbatim extracts from the novel—in other words, if the play regarded as a *book* is a colourable imitation of the novel.

<small>2 Blatch, 46.</small>

<small>Warne v. Seebohm, 39 Ch.D. 73.</small>

Again, we shall find later, when we come to discuss musical copyright, that if C makes a pianoforte score of the music of D's opera, C is in law the "author" of the new arrangement. So too if E writes new words and accompaniments to an old non-copyright melody, the whole composition is now a new one, and is copyright, E being rightly described as the author.

<small>Wood v. Boosey, 2 Q.B. 340.</small>

<small>Leader v. Purday, 7 C.B. 4.</small>

Joint authorship takes place where two or more agree to write a piece, the design and whole plan of which is the product of their joint intellectual labour, irrespective of the amount of work of composition actually performed by each. Thus, if A and B jointly determine to write a play on a subject jointly selected, or mutually agreed upon, and the scheme and arrangement are jointly discussed and settled, A and B are joint authors—presumably even if A does the whole of the literary composition.

"In order to constitute joint authorship of a dramatic piece or other literary work, it must be the result of a preconcerted joint design; mere alterations, additions, or improvements by another person, whether with or without the sanction of the author, will not entitle him to be called joint author." *Levy v. Rutley* L.R. 6, C.P. 529.

Again, where one person employs another to write a play and suggests a subject or scenes, but "has no share in the execution of the work, the whole of which, so far as any character for originality belongs to it, flows from the mind of the person employed, it appears an abuse of terms to say that the employer is the 'author' of a work to which he has not contributed an idea." *Per Jervis C.J. in Shepherd v. Conquest,* 17 C.B 427. It is clear what is here meant, though the closing sentence is rather unfortunate. A man who has suggested a subject or scenes can hardly be said not to have "contributed an idea." At the same time, he may not have shared in the general design or execution of the work, and in that case clearly is not a joint author.

As between the collaborateurs themselves, however, it may not be so easy to settle what is joint authorship. Thus, suppose A and B write a play jointly in the sense above given, but one particular scene is entirely the suggestion of A, and is in fact his only contribution to the joint production. When the play is produced, this particular scene, in deference to the protests of critics, is removed bodily from the play. Is A still to be regarded as joint author with B, and entitled to share the profits of representation? A, of course, would say "Yes;" B would probably say "No." There is little doubt that the law would pronounce in favour of A.

DRAMATISATION OF NOVELS AND OTHER WORKS.

A novel, and indeed any literary work not dramatic in form, becomes, when published, common property for dramatic purposes. Anybody may dramatise it and acquire a right of representation in the drama thus made. As pointed out in the Report of the Royal Commission on Copyright, 1876, p. xvi, "the practice has given rise to much complaint, and considerable loss, both in money and reputation, is alleged to have been inflicted upon novelists. The author's pecuniary injury consists in his failing to obtain the profit he might receive if dramatisation could not take place without his consent. He may be injured in reputation if an erroneous impression be given of his book."

The only way of obtaining the desired protection is for the author of the novel or other work to dramatise it himself, and publicly represent his dramatic composition before publishing his book.

Reade v. Conquest, 11 C.B.N.S. 479.

The case of Warne v. Seebohn illustrates so fully how far a playwright may trench upon the rights of a novelist, and at what point he is restrained, that no further apology seems needed for a rather more detailed discussion than this book purports to give of judicial decisions.

Warne v. Seebohn, 39 Ch.D. 73.

In Warne v. Seebohn, the defendant dramatised the story "Little Lord Fauntleroy," the property of the plaintiff, and caused his play to be performed upon the stage. It was not contended that he was not

39 Ch.D. 73.

entitled to do this. An author, when once he has published a novel or tale, has no exclusive right to it for purposes of dramatisation. Anyone may use it for that purpose. The infringement in this case complained of was that the defendant had multiplied copies of the plaintiff's tale; that for the purposes of producing the play he had made four copies, three for the actors and one for inspection and approval by the Licenser of Plays. No reliance was had upon Section 15 of the Copyright Amendment Act, which provides a remedy for infringement, where the infringement is limited to "printed" books, and books "exposed for sale or hire." Had there been such reliance, the plaintiff must have failed, since the defendant had not "printed" the copies, nor had he "exposed them for sale or hire." He relied simply upon his general rights in virtue of the Interpretation Clause of the Copyright Amendment Act, and of the undisputed judicial decision in Jeffreys *v.* Boosey that copyright is the sole liberty to print or *otherwise* multiply copies. The question therefore was, not whether the defendant had violated any acting or performing rights vested in the plaintiff, for the plaintiff had no such exclusive rights; nor whether the defendant was or was not entitled to dramatise plaintiff's tale, for the tale once published was common property as far as dramatisation is concerned.; but the point to be settled was whether the "book" of the play was an infringement of the copyright in the "book," "Little Lord Fauntleroy."

5 & 6 Vict., c. 45, s. 15.

5 & 6 Vict., c. 45.

4 H.L. Cas. 815.

The question was, therefore, a question of fact. Had the defendant in his "book"—that is in the four copies which he had made for the practical purpose of production on the stage—had he or had he not taken such a substantial part of plaintiff's "book" as to amount to an infringement of copyright proper? It was found that he had extracted almost verbatim from the tale very considerable passages for introduction into his play. Thus, Act I. consisted of 674 lines; 47 of these were stage directions; of the remaining 627, 125 were taken verbatim from the novel. Some of the passages extracted were prominent and striking parts of the dialogue contained in the novel. It was held that the copies made by the defendant were an infringement of the plaintiff's copyright, and that he was entitled to an injunction to restrain the defendant from printing or otherwise multiplying copies of his play containing any passages from the plaintiff's book. It was held also that all passages from the plaintiff's book in the four copies made must be cancelled.

It will be noticed that the defendant is not restrained from printing or otherwise multiplying copies of his play simply, but copies "containing any passages from the plaintiff's book." Such passages being cancelled, it appears that he can still make copies; and of his right to represent there can be no doubt.

Novelists will no doubt welcome this decision, as it gives them, though only by a side wind, a means of preventing in many cases the dramatisation of their works, since it places a practical impediment in the way of stage production. But the decision seems to leave the matter in a very unsatisfactory state. It practically says to the playwright, "You may take A's novel, make a play out of it, and represent it. But you must not make copies, however necessary for representation those copies may be, if they infringe the novelist's copyright in his book."

What, then, may the playwright take from the novel or tale of another? It does not appear to have been denied in Warne v. Seebohn that he may take, either for purposes of representation or of multiplying copies, title, plot, episodes, scenes and situations, bodily from the novel. No allusion was made to such appropriations in the order made. But if he takes a "certain amount" of the dialogue verbatim from the novel and introduces it into the copies of his play then he is infringing copyright.

Novelists and their sympathisers, and in the particular case the admirers of Mrs. Hodgson Burnett, may have rejoiced that a practical impediment was raised in the way of Mr. Seebohm, but the decision only serves to show how a logical and literal interpretation of the law may often be opposed to common sense. If the representation of a play constructed from the novel of another is no legal wrong to the novelist (and that is admitted) how can it be seriously said that the making of a few copies for stage purposes interferes with the sale of the book? Will the public who buy the *book* buy one copy the less because copies of the *play* have been made?

The novelist, if he is to be protected at all, should be protected as the Royal Commissioners suggest in their Report (p. xvi.), by statute, as the dramatist and musical composer are protected, and this could easily be accomplished by giving him the exclusive right of representation in addition to the right of multiplying copies which he already possesses. He should not be compelled to resort to such contemptible side issues as were raised, and raised successfully, in Warne *v.* Seebohm. 39 Ch.D. 73.

The author of novels and other literary works suffers in another respect. He cannot restrain recitations and readings from his works. Neither the Dramatic Copyright Amendment Act nor the Copyright Amendment Act appears to give to authors or assignees of novels or other literary works, not being dramatic, any right to restrain recitations or readings from them, unless the piece recited or read can be shown to be a "dramatic entertainment," though, of course, copies of the pieces read and recited cannot be multiplied and distributed without the consent of the author, for this would be to infringe copyright proper.

3 & 4 Wm. IV., c. 15.
5 & 6 Vict., c. 45.

WHAT IS A DRAMATIC COMPOSITION?

The words of the statute are "any Tragedy, Comedy, Play, Opera, Farce, or any other dramatic piece or entertainment." The cases show that a wide interpretation is to be given to the term "dramatic entertainment." In Russell *v.* Smith the Court held that "a song descriptive of the burning of a ship at sea, and the escape of those on board, and expressing in the supposed words of the sufferers, their feelings in strong language, was 'dramatic.'" In Lee *v.* Simpson it was held that the written introduction to a pantomime was a dramatic entertainment within the Act. In Chatterton *v.* Cave, that scenic effects and spectacular arrangements are within the Interpretation Clause of the Act.

<small>3 & 4 Wm. IV., c.15, s.1.</small>
<small>12 Q.B. 217.</small>
<small>3 C.B. 871.</small>
<small>10 C.P. 572.</small>
<small>5 & 6 Vict., c. 45.</small>

The ruling in Russell *v.* Smith is valuable in that it settles that a monologue may be a dramatic entertainment—in other words, that the popular view that it takes two performers at least to make a dramatic entertainment is, at any rate in law, erroneous. But it leaves unsettled, except by presumption and inference, such question as whether the recitation of Tennyson's "Northern Farmer," for example, is a dramatic entertainment.

It is suggested that the true meaning of dramatic entertainment is where the performer assumes a personality other than his own. According to this view, a recitation of the "Northern Farmer" would be a "dramatic entertainment," because—whether the reciter is in the costume of the place and period or not, whether he has the accessories of scenery or not, he for the time being *is* the Northern Farmer. But a recitation of "Enoch Arden" would not be such an entertainment, because the reciter is simply telling the author's story for him.

It may be objected on the principle *de minimis non*

curat lex, that as the Legislature has made provision for those compositions which, beyond argument or quibble, are "dramatic," compositions on the border-line can very well be left alone. Such an objection, however, is hardly fair in the face of the increasing popularity and remunerative nature of public readings and recitations.

It may not be out of place to note that the word "any" Tragedy, Comedy, &c., must be taken with a modification. The ruling that there is no copyright in an immoral, irreligious, seditious, or libellous composition, applies equally to dramatic works. It would therefore appear to be a good defence to an action for infringement to plead "no copyright" in the plaintiff, on the ground of the nature of the composition. It is, however, hardly conceivable that opportunity for such a pleading would occur, since no play can be performed without the licence of the Lord Chamberlain, and it is precisely to prevent the production of immoral or scurrilous plays that such licence is required by the Legislature. The extent to which this check may be exercised is illustrated by the action of the Licenser of Plays in regard to a burlesque representation by Mr. F. Leslie, at the Gaiety Theatre, of Mr. Henry Irving.

Walcot v. Walker, 7 Ves. 1.

WHAT IS A PLACE OF DRAMATIC ENTERTAINMENT?

In order to bring an authorised representation of a dramatic work within the statute, it is necessary to show that the representation has been given at "a place of dramatic entertainment." It, therefore, becomes necessary to ask what constitutes such a place. In Russell *v.* Smith the Master of the Rolls held that the nature of the performance determined the character of the place, and that *The Ship on Fire* being a dramatic entertainment, the place where it was performed

2 & 4 Wm. IV., c. 15.

12 Q.B. 217.

was a " place of dramatic entertainment." But the dictum was repudiated by the Master of the Rolls in Duck v. Bates, which therefore remains the leading case on this question.

<small>13 Q.B.D. 843.</small>

In that case the defendant and others joined in representing a dramatic piece in a room of a hospital without the consent of the proprietors of the copyright. The performance was merely for the entertainment of the nurses, attendants, and others connected with the hospital, who were admitted free of charge.

It was held by Brett, M.R., and Bowen, L.J. (Fry, L.J., dissenting), that the room where the drama was represented was not a place of public entertainment, and therefore the defendant was not liable to damages or penalties under ss. 1 & 2 of the statute.

<small>3 & 4 Wm. IV., c. 15.</small>

The question was—Is a place not ordinarily used for dramatic or any entertainments, and not used on the particular occasion for profit, a "place of dramatic entertainment" so as to bring the performance within the meaning of the Act? Two points, at least, are settled in the judgment given: (1) "It is not necessary," said the Master of the Rolls, " that there should be profit made by the representation." (2) The place need not be habitually kept for the exhibition of dramatic entertainments. A representation in a nursery by children, or by grown-up persons in a drawing-room, is not an infringement, because it is obviously domestic and private. So, too, "a representation for the amusement of friends in an unfurnished house hired for the occasion." The representation in that case also is "domestic and private." There must be present a sufficient part of the public who would also go to a performance licensed by the author as a commercial transaction. Suppose a member for a Parliamentary borough organises dramatic entertainments, to which the inhabitants are admitted without payment. Suppose an amateur company act some drama for a charitable object, with admission upon payment of money or by tickets issued generally. In each of these instances an infringement of the statute has been committed. Bowen, L.J., concurred.

Fry, L.J., while agreeing that the place need not be habitually used for dramatic entertainments, and that the representation need not be for reward or hire, differed as to the necessity for publicity, holding that "there may be internal and domestic representations which are well within the purview of the statute, as when a nobleman gives a dramatic performance in his mansion to guests staying in his house and to invited residents in the neighbourhood. What would be the chance of the next company, which came to the adjoining town to perform the same piece, getting together as good an audience as they could get had the piece not been performed in the nobleman's mansion?"

This appears to be the sounder view, and the only practical test as to what is a place of dramatic entertainment is whether the representation diminishes the pecuniary gains of the proprietor of the copyright.

The net result of these judgments is that three learned judges have held that to constitute a place of dramatic entertainment it is not necessary that it should be a place habitually used for such entertainments, nor need it be used on the particular occasion for profit; that two of the same three authorities have held that "publicity" is essential, while the third holds that it is not.

The case of Shelley *v.* Bethell, though raising a totally different point, gives some assistance in arriving at the judicial definition of a place of dramatic entertainment. In that case "the appellant was the owner and occupier of a building which he gratuitously allowed to be used on a few occasions for the performance of stage plays, to which the public were admitted on payment, for the benefit of a charity. The

12 Q.B.D. 11.

appellant had no licence for the performance of stage plays in the said building. Held that he was rightly convicted of having or keeping a house for the public performance of stage plays without a licence, under 6 & 7 Vict., c. 68, s. 2.

HOW THE RIGHT OF REPRESENTATION IS TRANSFERRED.

<small>Layland v. Stewart, L.R., 4 C.D. 419.

Marsh v. Conquest, 17 C.B.N.S. 418.

Cumberland v. Copeland, 7 H. & N. 118.</small>

For the present it is enough to say that assignment must be in writing, parol assignment being insufficient. But the writing need not be under seal, nor is attestation necessary, according to the rule laid down in Cumberland v. Copeland, over-ruling previous decisions.

Assignment by entry in Book of Register at Stationers' Hall as provided by the Copyright Amendment Act will be explained below, as also assignment by operation of the law.

INFRINGEMENT AND REMEDY.

Section 2 provides that every person who, without the consent in writing of the proprietor .... represents or causes to be represented at any place of dramatic entertainment in the British Dominions any dramatic piece or part thereof, shall pay to the proprietor "for each and every representation an amount not less than 40s., or the full amount of advantage arising from such representation, or the injury or loss sustained by the plaintiff therefrom, whichever may be the greater damages."

<small>3 & 4 Wm. IV.,c. 15, s.2.</small>

The infringement here provided for may consist, as was pointed out by James L.J., in Dicks v. Yates, in "open piracy" of the whole or part of a play, as when A represents B's drama without B's consent, giving out that B is the author.

<small>18 C.D. 76.</small>

Copyright is also infringed by what the same learned judge distinguished by the name of "literary larceny," or plagiarism, as where A takes the whole or a part of B's drama, and represents it as his (A's) composition. Whatever be the precise nature of the infringement, the remedy is the same.

But no action will lie unless the part taken is a substantial and material part. "The words 'production or any part thereof' must receive a reasonable construction, and are to be treated as implying some part that is substantial and material." It must be "a part and not a particle" that is taken, to constitute infringement. <small>Chatterton v. Cave, 3 App.C. 483.</small>

What amounts to an unlawful representation is a question of fact—for the jury. In Planché v. Braham, the performance of two or three songs out of the plaintiff's libretto without his consent was held to be an unlawful representation. <small>Planché v. Braham, 8 C. & P. 68.</small> This decision turned upon the amount represented, and did not touch the kindred question, what character of performance constitutes a representation. There are rehearsals, performances by marionettes, optical illusions, recitations in costume with scenic effects, and so forth. Are these "representations" within the meaning of the statute?

WHAT IS CONSENT WITHIN THE ACT?

The consent must be in writing. Any doubt as to this is removed by the decision in Eaton v. Lake, reversing the judgment of the Divisional Court and following that of Shepherd v. Conquest. <small>20 Q.B.D. 378. 17 C.B. 427.</small> "Oral permission to perform is not sufficient to constitute a binding assignment or consent to representation of a composition." But it need not necessarily be in the handwriting of or signed by the proprietor of the copyright. Thus, permission given by the secretary of a Dramatic Authors' Society to perform plays composed by members of the society is a sufficient consent within the Act—the secretary being the agent of the society, and thus of the individual members, in and for those purposes for which the society has been formed. Where two or more authors have collaborated, the consent of all must be obtained, for though there may be what is called a literary partnership, one partner cannot in this matter bind the other or others.

<small>Morton v. Copeland, 16 C.B. 517.</small>

<small>Powell v. Head, W.N. 1879, 86.</small>

WHO IS AN OFFENDER WITHIN THE ACT?

The words of the statute are "all who represent or cause to be represented." Some idea may be gathered from the following illustrations:—

(1) A, the proprietor of a tavern, let a room in the same to B, who gave an entertainment there. A, though informed that the pieces performed were being performed without the author's consent, allowed the entertainment to be given. It was held that his conduct did not amount to representing or causing to be represented, and that though the manager might be liable, he was not.

<small>Russell v. Briant, 8 C.B. 836.</small>

(2) C was the licensed proprietor of a theatre. D hired it for a dramatic entertainment which was in fact unauthorised. D brought his own company, had the selection of the pieces which were played, managed and controlled the performances, and all the persons engaged. C paid for printing and advertising, furnished the lighting power, doorkeepers, scene-shifters and supernumeraries, and hired the band, music being a necessary element in the performance. The money taken at the door was taken by C's servants. C retained one

half of the gross receipts as his remuneration for the use of the theatre, D taking the other half. It was held in an action by L for unauthorised performance of two plays of which he had the sole right of representation, that C had not "represented" the play, within the meaning of the Act, and that there was no partnership between him and D, so as to render him liable for the representation by D. Lyons *v.* Knowles, 10 L.T.N.S. 876.

(3) E was the licensed proprietor of a theatre, having a company, scenery, and effects of his own. He let the theatre fully equipped to F, together with the services of his company. An unauthorised performance was given by F. It was held that E had "caused the piece to be represented, and was consequently an offender within the meaning of the Act." The defendant here was owner of the dramatic company (which he was not in the previous case.) "He, therefore, I think, caused such piece to be performed." *Per* Erle, C.J. *in* Marsh *v.* Conquest, 10 Jur. N.S. 989.

THE NATURE OF THE SUM RECOVERABLE BY THE INJURED PARTY.

Choice is given: either (1) 40s. for each unauthorised performance; or (2) the amount of the benefit derived by the offender; or (3) the amount of injury sustained by the proprietor.

In the margin of the Act, the sum of 40s. is described as a "penalty." But it is not so in the common sense of the term. It was held in Adams *v.* Batley, and Cole *v.* Francis, that the section does not impose a penalty upon the offender so as to preclude the plaintiff, in an action to recover the specified 3 & 4 Wm. IV., c. 15.

18 Q.B.D. 625.

amount, from administering interrogatories to the defendant.
"The word 'offender' is only used as a convenient expression, and is in no way meant to designate
a criminal. . . . I am of opinion that this sum
of 40s. is not a penalty."

Per Day, J.

This decision of the Queen's Bench Division was affirmed on appeal, when Lord Esher, M.R., said : " I see no characteristic of a penalty in this payment. I am of opinion that this case is not brought within any rule of law which prevents interrogatories from being administered to the defendant."

The provision for double costs of suit has been repealed by 5 & 6 Vict., c. 97, s. 2.

When we come to discuss Musical Copyright in the following chapter, we shall find that important alterations in the law as to Penalties and Costs have been made by 45 & 46 Vict., c. 40, s. 4, and 51 & 52 Vict., c. 17, but only so far as musical compositions are concerned. For the unlawful representation of dramatic compositions, the provisions of the Act of William IV. are still in force.

LIMITATION OF ACTION.

3 & 4 Wm. IV., c. 15, s. 3.

All proceedings for offences under this Act must be brought within twelve calendar months next after the committing of the same.

CHAPTER II.

MUSICAL AND DRAMATIC COPYRIGHT.

General Remarks—Who may Possess Copyright?—In what Copyright Exists—Duration of Copyright Proper—Duration of Performing Rights—Periodicals—Transfer of Rights—Registration—Delivery of Copies—Infringement—Remedies.

GENERAL REMARKS.

WE have seen in the preceding chapter that the Dramatic Copyright Act gave to the dramatic author what he did not before possess—the right of controlling the representation of his composition. *3 & 4 Wm. IV., c. 15.* This Act, however, did not extend to music except so far as a musical composition came within the category of dramatic pieces or entertainments. Thus, the composer of an opera would have had the benefits of the Act, while the composer of an instrumental piece would not. The case of a song would have depended upon showing that it was a "dramatic piece or entertainment." By the Copyright Amendment Act, commonly called Talfourd's Act, this "performing right" was extended to *5 & 6 Vict., c. 45.* composers of music of any kind, section 20 enacting that the provisions of the previous Act shall apply to musical compositions (without distinction), and section 21, that the person who shall have the sole liberty of representing any dramatic piece or musical composition, shall have and enjoy the remedies provided by 3 & 4 Wm. IV., c. 15, as if the same were re-enacted.

Copyright proper, that is the right of controlling the multiplication of copies, which existed prior to the Dramatic Copyright Act, was created anew and extended in duration by the Copyright Amendment Act. The contrast between copy- *3 & 4 Wm. IV., c. 15.* *5 & 6 Vict., c. 45.*

right proper, and the right of representation and performance, is clearly set forth in Chappell *v.* Boosey. "Under the Copyright Act of Anne, the author of a dramatic or musical composition acquired a copyright in his work, so as to be enabled to prevent any other person from multiplying copies of it. . . . By the Interpretation Clause of the Copyright Amendment Act, the word 'book' is made to include every sheet of letterpress and sheet of music, and the word 'dramatic piece' is made to include every scenic, musical, or dramatic entertainment. Therefore, in virtue of this Act (*i.e.*, the Copyright Amendment Act), a dramatic author and musical composer have a double right, viz.:—

margin: Chappell v. Boosey, 21 Ch.D. 232.
margin: 8 Anne, c. 19.

(1) Copyright proper, preventing the multiplication of copies of the piece itself.

(2) What may be called the acting or performing right, conferring the power of preventing other persons from publicly representing or performing the piece without consent.

These rights are quite distinct, each being separate property, and each capable of being assigned without the other, and of expiring at different times."

margin: Per North, J., in Chappell v. Boosey, 21 Ch.D. 232.

Following the plan of the preceding chapter, it is now proposed to discuss the various questions which arise upon the construction of the different sections of the last-mentioned Act.

margin: 5 & 6 Vict., c. 45.

WHO MAY POSSESS COPYRIGHT?

"The word 'author' is used (in the Copyright Amendment Act as in the Dramatic Copyright Act) without limitation or restriction, and is therefore equally applicable to foreigners as to British subjects."

This was unanimously decided by the House of Lords in Routledge *v.* Low.

margin: 5 & 6 Vict., c. 45.
margin: 3 & 4 Wm. IV., c. 15.
margin: 3 Eng. & Ir. Ap. 100.

But while the term "author" is unlimited, the area of publication is restricted to the United Kingdom.

"The first publication of a book must, to secure British copyright to its author, be made in the United Kingdom." Ibid.

This likewise was a unanimous decision, as also that "British Copyright," when once it exists, extends over every part of the British Dominions, which by the Interpretation Clause of the Copyright Amendment Act means future as well as present possessions of the British Crown.

The question whether protection will be extended to a foreigner who has published in the United Kingdom, but who is resident out of the British Dominions, cannot yet be said to be settled. In Routledge v. Low the point was not expressly raised, though the learned judges expressed their opinions upon it. But those opinions were not unanimous. Lord Cairns said: "Protection is given to every author who publishes in the United Kingdom, *wheresoever that author may be resident*, or of whatever State he may be the subject." Lord Westbury, rejecting the decision in Jeffreys v. Boosey, as "not a binding authority in the exposition of this later statute," speaking to the same effect as Lord Cairns, said: "The real condition of obtaining its advantages is the first publication by the author of his work in the United Kingdom. Nothing renders necessary his bodily presence here at the time." Lords Cranworth and Chelmsford, however, adhered to the rule laid down in Jeffreys v. Boosey, and it was authoritatively decided that "to entitle a foreigner to copyright in any work first published by him in the United Kingdom he must be actually resident." 4 H.L. Cas. 815.

Though the question of residence cannot be considered settled, there is no doubt that publication must take place in the United Kingdom as a condition precedent to protection. But even this is modified by the Colonial Copyright

Acts (dealt with elsewhere), and generally all that is said as to rights of foreigners in British dominions, and rights of British subjects in foreign dominions, must be taken subject to the modifications introduced by International Copyright Acts, by Orders in Council and Conventions, a full account of which is given in subsequent chapters.

It will be understood that what has been here said of the "author" applies with equal force to any person to whom the author has legally assigned his rights.

IN WHAT COPYRIGHT MAY EXIST.

There is no copyright in a piracy, on the principle that the pirate's "hands are not clean." For a reason similar there is no copyright in an obscene or libellous work. There is apparently no copyright in any work calculated to mislead or defraud the public.

<small>Stockdale v. Onwhyn, 5 B. & C. 173.</small>

<small>Gounod v. Hutchings. Gounod v. Wood. "Times," Nov. 22, 1872.</small>

There is no copyright in a title which is not original, nor in one that relates to a projected but non-existing work.

<small>Dicks v. Yates, 18 Ch.D. 76.</small>

<small>Maxwell v. Hogg, 16 L.T.N.S. 130.</small>

The leading case as to this question is Weldon v. Dicks. Malins, V.C., reviewing Maxwell v. Hogg, said: "Lord Cairns expressed an opinion that there could be no copyright in a name. It must be borne in mind that he was dealing with a case in which Mr. Hogg had nothing but the name (he had registered the title of a projected magazine), and it had not been followed up by publication. But if he had published one number on September 1st (the entered date) under the title of 'Belgravia,' it is plain the name would have been protected as decided in the case of Bradbury v. Beeton. But to say that there is no title in a name as a part of a publication, newspaper, book, or periodical is in my opinion entirely absurd."

<small>10 Ch.D. 247. 16 L.T.N.S. 130.</small>

<small>39 L.J., Ch. 57.</small>

At the present day, when the value of a title is very

considerable, the above ruling is of extreme importance. The propositions which may be extracted from it appear to be as follows:—
  (1) There is copyright in a title provided it is original, and provided it relates to an existing work, and not one merely in contemplation;
  (2) Its registration will avail provided that at the date entered as that of first publication the work to which the title is applied is published; but
  (3) There is no copyright in a title only, so that it is impossible to secure a title by registration by way of anticipation.

This last proposition presents what is felt by authors as a serious grievance. An author having commenced a composition, and having hit upon a striking title—a matter of great difficulty and value—has no means of securing the title till his work is complete.

There is copyright in new words and accompaniments written to an old, *i.e.* non-copyright, air. This was settled in the case of Leader *v.* Purday. Bellamy wrote new words to an old non-copyright melody, called "Pestal," and got a composer (Horne) to compose an accompaniment. It was held that he acquired copyright in both words and accompaniment, and that his assignee in declaring for an infringement may describe himself as proprietor of the copyright in the whole composition. A similar ruling was given in the later case of Lover *v.* Davidson. 7 C.B. 4

1 C.B.N.S. 182.

Samuel Lover wrote the words entitled "The Low-backed Car" to an old (non-copyright) melody—"The Jolly Ploughboy." It was held that "one who adapts words of his own to an old air, adding thereto a prelude and accompaniment also of his own, acquires a copyright in the combination." In both these cases it will be observed the new combination consists of the old melody, new words and new accompaniment. There is no case on the question whether new words, adapted to an old melody and the old accompaniment, give copyright in the new combination, but there can be little doubt that the same principle would apply.

The law with regard to adapting new words to non-copyright music is very similar to that relating to the dramatising of novels. For dramatic purposes a novel, once published, becomes public property, and any person may dramatise it, provided any copies which he makes of his play do not as a *book* infringe the copyright in the novel. But the author of the play first produced cannot prevent others from utilising the same novel for dramatic purposes so long as recourse is had to the novel, which is common property, and not to his play, which is private property.

<small>Warne v. Seebohm, 39 Ch.D. 73.</small>

So too, though any person may adapt new words to a non-copyright melody and obtain copyright in the new combination, he may not prevent other persons from using the same melody. Thus the melody of a modern Irish ballad entitled "Father O'Flynn" is non-copyright, and therefore common property. But there is copyright in the new combination of words and music called "Father O'Flynn."

The same remarks apply to the more important case of writing libretti to the music of non-copyright operas, oratorios, or cantatas.

Where the copyright has expired, or where it is not protected by any Acts or Conventions, there appears to be nothing to prevent a person from adapting a new libretto to the music, and obtaining copyright in the new combination.

Thus if a Russian produce and publish an opera in Russia, an English librettist might adapt a libretto to it and obtain British copyright therein to the exclusion of the Russian composer, though he could not prevent another

English librettist from making a like use of the music. So it would be conceivable that there might be two simultaneous representations of a new opera at rival houses, the only difference between them being in the libretti. Russia is taken as an illustration because not within the provisions of the International Copyright Act and the Conventions. As a matter of fact, however, the great Russian composers of the day obtain protection by publishing in some country which has subscribed to the Berne Convention.

Copyright is also gained in an authorised arrangement for the piano (and, apparently, for any instrument) of quadrilles, waltzes, and other dances from the melodies of an opera, because of the individual intellectual labour involved in making the same; and the adapter and not the composer of the opera is in the event of registration to be entered as the "composer" of the arrangement. *Attwill v. Ferritt, 2 Blatch. Amer. 39. D'Almaine v. Boosey, 1 Y. & C. 288.*

There is also copyright in the complete score of an opera arranged for a pianoforte, whether arranged by the composer himself or by another. The pianoforte arrangement is regarded as a work separate from the opera itself, and as the result of separate labour. There is also copyright in translations. "A man has a copyright in a translation upon which he has bestowed his time and labour. To be sure, another man has an equal right to translate the original work and to publish his translation; but then it must be his own translation, by his own skill and labour, and not the mere use by publication of the translation already made by another." *Wood v. Boosey, L.R., 3 Q.B. 223. Per Justice Story in Emerson v. Davies, 3 St. Rep. 780.*

The law as to translations is of course qualified by the provisions of the International Copyright Act, Orders in Council, and Conventions.

Thus an unauthorised translation of an English copyright work into French, or of a French work into English, is an infringement of copyright; but an unauthorised French translation of an American or Russian work is no infringement, because America and Russia are not parties to the Berne Convention.

There is no copyright in a work at home if it is first published abroad. This was judicially settled in Clementi *v.* Walker, and Guichard *v.* Mori. It is now also a statutory enactment.

<small>2 B. & C. 861.
9 L.J.Ch.227
7 Vict., c. 12,
s. 19.</small>

But where publications at home and abroad are simultaneous, the home-copyright is not lost. In the case of Cocks *v.* Purday, "Der Elfinwaltzer," a composition by Joseph Labitsky was published in England and at Prague contemporaneously. It was held, in an action for infringement of copyright, that the plaintiff was entitled to recover.

<small>Cocks *v.* Purday,
2 Car. & Kirw. 269.</small>

The rule that copyright is lost by prior publication abroad also applies to the case of representation or performance of dramatic and musical compositions.

In Boucicault *v.* Delafield, the plaintiff having first produced his play, the *Colleen Bawn*, in New York, sought to restrain the defendant from producing it here. Wood, V.C., held that the production in New York was a publication within 7 Vict., c. 12, and that the plaintiff had consequently lost his copyright here. A similar point was raised in Boucicault *v.* Chatterton.

<small>1 H. & M.,
597.</small>

<small>5 Ch.D.
C.A. 272.</small>

In that case, the plaintiff claimed under the Dramatic Copyright Act, and contended that his rights were not affected by 7 Vict., c. 12, s. 19, that the play had not been published abroad, as representations had in an old case (Coleman *v.* Wathen) been held not to amount to publication. But Malins, V.C., considered himself bound by the ruling in Boucicault *v.* Delafield, and held that the play had been "published" within the meaning of 7 Vict., c. 12, s. 19, and therefore that

<small>3 & 4 Wm.
IV., c. 15.</small>

<small>5 T.R., 245.</small>

the plaintiff had lost his sole right of representation. James, L.J., said, "A book is published by being printed and issued to the public; a dramatic piece or a musical composition is published by being publicly performed. . . . I am of opinion that the decision of the Vice-Chancellor (Malins) is right." The ruling was confirmed.

It would appear, however, that representation of a play abroad is not such a publication of it as would destroy copyright in it as a book. For example, by representing the *Colleen Bawn* and the *Shaughran* in New York, Mr. Boucicault lost his exclusive right of representation in England, but did not lose his exclusive right of publishing those plays as books. Conversely it appears that publications of plays as books abroad is not such a publication as to destroy performing-rights at home. These are inferences from the undisputed proposition that right of representation and right of multiplying copies (*i.e.*, copyright proper) are "two separate and distinct rights." *Per* North, J. *in* Chappell *v.* Boosey, 21 Ch.D. 232.

DURATION OF COPYRIGHT PROPER.

The term of copyright in dramatic and musical compositions regarded as books, was, by virtue of 54 Geo. III., c. 156, for the life of the author, or for twenty-eight years from the date of publication, whichever period was the longer. This term was extended by the Copyright Amendment Act, which provided that when a book is published in the lifetime of its author, the copyright in it is the personal property of the author and his assigns from the date of such publication for forty-two years from publication, or "for the natural life of the author, and for a further term of seven years, commencing at the time of his death," provided that the period shall in no case be less than forty-two years; while if the publication takes place "after the author's death, the copyright shall endure 5 & 6 Vict., c. 45, s. 3.

for forty-two years from the first publication thereof." Thus, copyright must endure for forty-two years, while it may endure for more, *e.g.*, if A publish a book at twenty-one, and die at eighty, by the addition of the seven years, his copyright will endure for sixty-six years. The Royal Commissioners in their Report (1876), page x, mention various objections to the statutory period. First, it is said not to be long enough. As to this, the argument lies between those who support the pecuniary interests of authors, and those on the other hand who regard public benefit as of primary importance. The second objection is that copyrights belonging to the same author generally expire at different dates. The third is that it is usually difficult, if not impossible, to ascertain the termination of a copyright, owing to the fact that the expiration of the period depends upon the time of publication.

The date of a man's death can, in most cases, be easily ascertained. Not so the date of publication. What contributes to the difficulty is that registration at Stationers' Hall, though it is a condition precedent to suing, is not essential to the existence of copyright itself. The Commissioners' recommendation is that the period of copyright should last for the life of the author and a fixed number of years after his death; and the term adopted in Germany is suggested (viz., life and thirty years).

DURATION OF PERFORMING-RIGHTS.

The term of copyright provided by section 3, just mentioned is by section 20 applied to the right of representation and performance. The period is to be dated from first public representation or performance. In virtue, therefore, of these two sections taken in conjunction with the provisions of the Dramatic Copyright Act, dramatic authors and musical com-

5 & 6 Vict., c. 45, s. 3.

3 & 4 Wm. IV., c. 15.

posers are, as regards the duration of their rights, in a precisely similar position; and these rights are of two distinct kinds, viz., copyright proper and performing-rights, and may consequently reside in different persons simultaneously, and may expire at different periods.

DURATION OF COPYRIGHT IN THE CASE OF PERIODICALS.

The publication of dramatic and musical compositions in periodical form, or as parts of periodicals, is not, perhaps, of common occurrence. But the custom is sufficiently well established, and even seems to be so much on the increase that it appears necessary to say a few words on the law relating to such publications.

The law is contained in section 18 of the Copyright Amendment Act, "the short effect of which is to transfer for a *limited period a portion* of the copyright to the proprietor of the periodical for whom the article has been composed." 5 & 6 Vict., c. 45, s. 18.
Per Chitty, J. *in* Trade Auxiliary Co. *v.* Middlesborough & District Tradesmen's Protection Association, 40 Ch.D., 425, C.A.

The right of the publisher or proprietor endures for the period given by the Act to the authors of books, viz., the natural life and seven years beyond, or at the least, forty-two years from date of publication. This is provided in terms by the section (18). But the right is limited in this way, that the proprietor is precluded from publishing in separate form, without the consent of the author, compositions written by the latter for, and published in, such periodical, "the reason obviously being that the author would be seriously injured if being minded at the end of twenty-eight years to publish his writings separately or in a collected form, he should find that they had been already published separately from the periodical work to which they were contributed." *Per* Page Wood, V.C., *in* Mayhew *v.* Maxwell, 1 Johns & H. 315.

After the expiration of twenty-eight years the right of

separate publication reverts to the author for the residue of the allotted period, viz., the forty-two years, or the rest of his natural life, and seven years beyond. Thus there may be on sale to the public the same composition as a separate publication published by the author or his assigns, and as a part of a periodical or collection published by the proprietor of the periodical, neither publication infringing the other. The rights of both persons expire simultaneously, *i.e.*, at the expiration of forty-two years from first publication, or seven years from the death of the author.

In order that section 18 should apply it is necessary that the work should have been composed upon the terms (express or implied) that the copyright therein shall belong to the proprietor as to the author of a book, and that the price bargained for shall have been paid.

<small>Richardson v. Gilbert, 20 L. J. (Ch.) 553.</small>

In addition to the right given by section 18 to authors to restrain the proprietor of the periodical from publishing their contributions separately, they may also by express contract reserve to themselves the right to publish them separately during the twenty-eight years, in which case the copyright in the separate publication belongs to them, but without prejudice to the proprietor of the periodical.

If the contribution be pirated by a third party, the author, according to the view of the Royal Commissioners, apparently has no right to take proceedings until the right of separate publication has reverted to him, *i.e.*, after twenty-eight years from first publication, "so that unless the proprietor of the magazine or periodical be willing to take such proceedings, which may very likely not be the case when the right of the author is about to revive, the result would practically be to deprive the author of the benefit of the right reserved to him."

<small>Report of the R.C. 1876, par. 44.</small>

These remarks apparently do not apply when authors, by express contract with the proprietors of the periodical, reserve to themselves the right of separate publication, for in that case the copyright in the contribution as a separate publication belongs to them, and they are consequently in the same position as ordinary copyright-holders, and all that they have parted with to the proprietor of the periodical is the right to use their contributions.

Authors who contribute to magazines and periodicals would do well to consider this question, and more especially authors of verses, not because they are of more importance than other compositions, but because, if suitable for setting to music, various peculiar difficulties may arise.

Suppose such a set of verses be composed for a magazine upon the terms mentioned in section 18 of the Copyright Amendment Act, and paid for; the copyright in the verses vests in the proprietor of the magazine. Assume that nothing has been specified in the terms of the contract as to musical setting, or as to reservation of the right of separate publication. The verses, having been published in the periodical, are set to music and published separately by the proprietor of the periodical. Clearly this is an infringement of the right conveyed by section 18. But if anyone else publishes them with music, without the consent of the proprietor of the periodical, it would appear, according to the view of the Royal Commissioners above quoted, that the author cannot sue until the expiration of the twenty-eight years, though probably the proprietor can.

If, however, by express contract the author has reserved the right of separate publication, then he has copyright, and can sue at once upon any infringement.

TRANSFER OF COPYRIGHT.

In reference to literary and artistic copyright, an assign is defined as "every person in whom the interest of an author in copyright is vested, whether derived from such author before or after publication." 5 & 6 Vict., c. 45, s. 2.

This transfer of rights takes place—
  (a) By operation of the law.
  (b) By act of party.

(a) Copyright, being personal property, passes on intestacy to the personal representatives of the author or proprietor, and on bankruptcy to the trustees for the benefit of the creditors. It has been stated in an able work upon copyright that, though the copyright in works that are printed and published will legally pass to the trustees in bankruptcy, it does not pass in the case of manuscripts, and the reason assigned for the distinction is that the author's right of withholding publication continues till the very moment his book is actually given to the public. The cases, however, which the learned writer cites in support of his proposition, do not seem to support it. It is true that it has been held both in America and this country that unpublished manuscripts do not pass by seizure under an execution. But this is not the same thing as saying that manuscripts do not pass to the trustees in bankruptcy. There is, in fact, authority for the contrary proposition. In Longman v. Tripp it was held that the right to publish a newspaper will pass to the trustees in bankruptcy even under the words of the older Bankruptcy Acts, and since the recent statute of 1883 contains a more comprehensive vesting clause than any preceding Act, it would seem that there can now be no doubt on this question.

marginalia: 5 & 6 Vict., c. 45, s. 25. Copinger, 157. 2 Bos. & Pull. New. 67. 46 & 47 Vict., c. 52, ss. 44 & 68.

(b) Copyright is transferred by act of party—
  (1) By assignment, which is either express or implied.
  (2) By licence.

(1) Assignment is express where by sale or gift the author or proprietor transfers in terms his rights to another. Such a transfer must be in writing. But, as already pointed

out, it need not be under seal, nor according to the latest decision is attestation necessary.

Any words will suffice, provided they will clearly express intention to transfer the rights. Thus, where A wrote to B that he would "let B have" a drama belonging to him (A) in discharge of so much owing by A to B, this was held to be a complete assignment. Again, where A commissioned B to compose music as an accessory to a dramatic piece (which A was preparing for production), on terms that in consideration of payment the music should be a part of the dramatic piece, and A should have the sole liberty of representing it, the music was held to be the property of A.

Lacey *v.* Toole, 15 L.T.N.S. 512.

Hatton *v.* Kean, 7 C.B. N.S. 268.

Assignment is implied where one person employs and pays another to write a "book" on the terms that the copyright therein shall belong to the employer. This is in substance the effect of section 18 of the Copyright Amendment Act. It has often been objected that the wording of the section with reference to payment is ungrammatical. It is, however, not necessary to review or contest this objection since there is clear authority for the meaning of the section. In Richardson *v.* Gilbert it was held that "under 5 & 6 Vict., c. 45, s. 18, actual payment for an article (which presumably includes dramatic and musical compositions) written for a periodical work, is a condition precedent to the vesting of the copyright in the proprietor of the work. A contract for payment is not sufficient."

5 & 6 Vict., c. 45, s. 18.

20 L.J. (Ch.) 553.

Nor is payment alone sufficient to vest copyright. In Walter *v.* Howe it was held that "to enable the proprietor of a newspaper to sue in respect of a piracy of any article therein, he must show not merely that the author of the article has been paid for his services, but that it has been composed on the terms that the copyright therein shall belong to such proprietor."

17 Ch.D. 708.

These terms, however, need not be expressed, but may be implied.

Thus if A, the proprietor of a Christmas number of a periodical, requests B to compose a song, play, or instrumental piece, naming only a price, and making no mention of copyright, and B agrees, the copyright in the composition vests in A on payment by him to B of the stipulated price.

"Though no express words are stated, I think that where a man employs another to write an article or to do anything else for him, unless there is something in the surrounding circumstances or in the course of dealing between the parties to require a different construction, in the absence of a specified agreement to the contrary, it is to be understood that the writing or other thing is produced upon the terms that the copyright therein shall belong to the employer."

Sweet v. Benning, 16 C.B., 459.

Copyright may be also assigned by entry in the Register Book of Stationers' Hall.

When it is desired to adopt this course, the proprietor must himself be registered in the following form :—

TIME OF MAKING THE ENTRY.	TITLE OF BOOK.	NAME OF PUBLISHER AND PLACE OF PUBLICATION.	NAME AND PLACE OF ABODE OF PROPRIETOR OF COPYRIGHT.	DATE OF FIRST PUBLICATION.

5 & 6 Vict., c. 45, s. 13.

For such entry he must pay the sum of 5s. to the officer of the Stationers' Company.

"Every registered proprietor may assign his interest or

any portion of his interest by making entry in the Book of Registry of such assignment, and of the name and place of abode of the assignee thereof." This is done in the following form:—

I, A B, of ————, being the Assigner of the Copyright of the Book hereunder described, do hereby require you to make entry of the assignment of the Copyright therein.

TITLE OF BOOK.	ASSIGNER OF COPYRIGHT	ASSIGNEE OF COPYRIGHT.

Dated this ———— day of —————, 18 .

(Signed)   —————.

The entry, which will be made upon payment of a further fee of 5s., should run as follows:—

DATE OF ENTRY.	TITLE OF BOOK.	ASSIGNER OF COPYRIGHT.	ASSIGNEE OF COPYRIGHT.

"Such assignment so entered shall be effectual in law to all intents and purposes whatsoever, without being subjected to any stamp or duty, and shall be of the same force and effect as if such assignment had been made by deed." It must not be inferred from the

<small>5 & 6 Vict., c. 45, s. 13.</small>

allusion to assignment by deed, that a deed is a necessary. It has been already pointed out, on the authority of Jeffreys *v.* Boosey, that assignment is effectual when not under seal.

<small>4 H.L. Cas. 891.</small>

Bearing in mind that in connection with every dramatic and musical composition there are two rights, viz., copyright proper and "performing-rights," we have now to inquire how far assignment of the former right will imply assignment of the latter. In Cumberland *v.* Planché it was held that where an author simply assigned the copyright of a composition, he also parted with the right of representation. This decision is met by section 22 of the Copyright Amendment Act, which enacts that "no assignment of copyright in any dramatic or musical composition shall convey to the assignee the right of representation or performance, unless an entry in the Registry Book of the Stationers' Company shall be made of such assignment, wherein shall be expressed the intention of the parties that such right (*i.e.*, the right of representation) shall pass by such assignment."

<small>1 A. & E. 580.</small>

<small>5 & 6 Vict., c. 45, s. 22.</small>

If we construe this section literally, it would appear that in order to vest the right of representation in an assignee, registration is necessary. And yet in section 24 of the same Act it is expressly provided "that nothing herein contained (as to registration) shall prejudice the remedies which the proprietor of the sole liberty of representing any dramatic piece shall have by virtue of the Act (3 & 4 Wm. IV., c. 15) or of this Act, although no entry shall be made in the Book of Registry aforesaid."

<small>5 & 6 Vict., c. 45, s. 24.</small>

Thus, according to section 22, registration is necessary, while according to section 24, it is unnecessary. Judicial decisions, however, show that section 22 is not to be construed literally. Thus where a composer assigned, without registration, for value all his present, future, and contingent copyright in a musical composition, and all other right, title, interest, property, contingency, it was held by the Court of Appeal to convey the exclusive right of performance as well as of printing and selling copies.

<small>Hutchins and Romer, ex pte. L.R., 4 Q.B.D. 483.</small>

This decision was doubtless given because of the wide and comprehensive terms employed—"all other right, title, interest, property, contingency." But in such an assignment as the following, it is conceived that the statute would be literally interpreted : " In consideration of the sum of £100, I hereby assign to A B the copyright in my drama entitled X Y. Signed, C D," and that such an assignment would convey no more than the right to print and publish the drama or musical composition as a " book."

The performing-rights not being transferred, the author or his assign can sue for unauthorised performances, and it is easy to see how vexatious proceedings may be taken. Such proceedings were in fact so frequently taken that fresh legislation was actually invoked, and Acts were passed by which it was provided that notwithstanding the provisions of the Dramatic Copyright Act and of the Copyright Amendment Act the Court may award a less sum than 40s. for each unauthorised performance, and where such less sum is awarded the costs shall be in the discretion of the Court.

<small>45 & 46 Vict., c. 40, and 51 & 52 Vict., c. 17.

3 & 4 Wm. IV., c. 15.

5 & 6 Vict., c. 45.</small>

The prospect of getting 1s. by way of damages and no costs can hardly be described as an incentive to litigation.

It only remains to add, on this question of the division of copyright and performing-rights, that as by section 22 of the Copyright Amendment Act an assignment of copyright, *i.e.*, right to multiply copies, does not convey to the assignee the right of representation or performance, so it may be presumed that a transfer of performing-rights will not of itself convey any

<small>5 & 6 Vict., c. 45, s. 2.</small>

rights to multiply copies. The two rights are, as already stated, separate and distinct.

Specimens of assignments are given in the Appendix, from which it will be seen that no difficulties or disputes with regard to the extent of the rights conveyed need occur as between author and publisher where the intentions of the parties are clearly and in terms set out.

Where an author desires to reserve any portion of such rights as he possesses at common law or by statute over his compositions, the instrument should take the form of a licence, and not an assignment, since an assignment implies transfer of all rights without reservation. Thus if a writer of words for musical setting desires to reserve the right to print and publish his words apart from and independently of music or musical purposes, he should not "assign" his copyright to the proprietor or publisher of the music, but should give a licence to print and publish with music, as well as in programmes or word-books of concerts, and to perform the same. Such a licence gives the publisher or proprietor of the music all the control that he desires, while it leaves to the author the right to control the publication of his words in any form other than "musical."

This distinction between licence and assignment has been clearly laid down in Reade *v.* Bentley, and in Taylor *v.* Neville. In the former case it was held in terms that "a licence to publish is not an assignment;" and in the latter, "a receipt for so much for the 'London right' of a play was held to be a license, and not an assignment." The only further point is the question whether a licensee can assign his interest just as an assignee can further assign his. This was also settled in Taylor *v.* Neville. "A licence is assignable." An acknowledgment by Taylor of the receipt of a sum of money from A and B for "the London right" of a play was held to be a licence or consent, giving to A and

_{4 K. & J., 656.}

_{38 L.T.N.S. 50.}

_{38 L.T.N.S. 50.}

B, for the whole period of Taylor's own right, the sole right to represent the play in London, and that such licence or consent was assignable by A and B.

REGISTRATION AT STATIONERS' HALL.

Registration is of importance not only as a means of assigning copyright, but also as a condition precedent to suing.

No proprietor may "maintain any action at law, or in equity, or any summary proceedings in respect of any infringement, unless before commencing such action or proceeding he shall have made an entry in the Book of Registry of the Stationers' Company," provided for by section 11 of the same Act. *5 & 6 Vict., c. 45, s. 24.*

In the case of the London Printing Alliance and Keep and Co. *v.* Cox, the question was whether the plaintiffs were duly registered proprietors of the copyright so as to be able to sue. Keep & Co. being owners of copyright in a picture called "On the Threshold," negotiated with the Alliance for the sale to them for publication in *Myra's Journal.* A letter of the 19th April, 1890, was written by Keep to the Alliance, which in the opinion of the majority of the Appeal Court amounted to an immediate assignment, and made the Alliance legal proprietors. *7 Times Reports, 738.*

The Alliance were never registered. Keep and Co. alone were on the register. It was held by two Judges of Appeal against one that an action by the Alliance and Keep and Co. for infringement by publication of the picture in the *Queen* was bad, as "the proprietor" was not on the register. Lord Justice Fry had no doubt that a trustee in whom the property was vested might be registered and sue, but one person could not be owner and another be registered and sue ; the registration of Keep and Co. was in fact held to be a nullity, as they had parted with their interest. Lord Justice Lindley, the one dissentient, considered that the letter only amounted to a conditional agreement to assign to the Alliance, on certain bills being given by them ; that Keep and Co. were trustees for the Alliance subject to the condition being performed, and were rightly registered and could sue. The Court only differed as to the construction of the letter of April 19th, and agreed as to the law that a trustee is a proprietor who may be registered and sue. It was not decided whether the persons beneficially interested might be registered in lieu of the trustee. It is apprehended that if the whole beneficial interest were represented on the register this would be good, and that the trustee, though a proper, is not a necessary subject for registration.

It will be noticed that omission to register does not affect copyright itself, but only the right to sue.

"It is not necessary for an author or publisher to register his work in order to be entitled to the copyright. But by section 24 of the Act (5 & 6 Vict., c. 45) he is bound to register his copyright before he can maintain an action or suit at law, or in equity, in respect of any infringement of such copyright. Therefore, before he sues he must register."

<small>Per Malins, V.C., in Weldon v. Dicks. L.R., 10 Ch.D., 252.</small>

There are, however, two cases in which an injured proprietor can sue for infringement, without previous registration.

The first is that of the unauthorised representation of a dramatic work. Section 24, which makes registration a condition precedent to suing, expressly provides that "nothing herein contained shall prejudice the remedies which the proprietor of the sole liberty of representing any dramatic piece shall have by virtue of the 3 Wm IV., c. 15 . . . although no entry shall be made in the Book of Registry aforesaid." In other words, the proprietor of the "performing-rights" in a dramatic piece may sue without registration.

Following out of this is the question whether what is settled as to a proprietor is equally true of an assignee; whether, that is, an assignee may sue without previous registration. On general grounds it would seem that there could be no doubt, an assignee being, in respect of remedies, precisely in the same position as the assignor. The doubt is caused by the fact that the proviso in section 24 exempts "the proprietor," and does not mention the assignee in terms as other sections (viz., 2, 9, 20) do.

There is, however, no longer any room for doubt since the decision in Marsh v. Conquest. "It is competent to the *assignee* of the sole right of representing a dramatic piece to sue for penalties under 3 & 4 Wm. IV., c. 15, notwithstanding the assignment is not by deed, or registered under the Copyright Amendment Act (5 & 6 Vict., c. 45)."

<small>17 C.B.N.S. 418.</small>

Proprietors and assignees of musical compositions may also sue for unlawful performances without previous registration. This is by virtue of the Interpretation Clause of the Copyright Amendment Act, by which "dramatic piece" is made to include a musical entertainment.

The second case in which an injured proprietor may sue for infringement without registration is that of the author of a composition published in a periodical. It will be remembered that in virtue of section 18 of 5 & 6 Vict., c. 45, the proprietor of the periodical may not publish the composition separately without the author's consent. Supposing he or any other person does so publish the composition, the author's rights are infringed. To sue for such infringement, separate registration by the author is not necessary. This is clear from the case of Mayhew or Murray *v.* Maxwell: "The right of an author of an article in a periodical under 5 & 6 Vict., c. 45, s. 18, to prevent a separate publication is not copyright within the meaning of section 24"— which requires registration prior to suing—"and it is no objection to a motion for an injunction in such a case that the author has not entered his work at Stationers' Hall." 1 Johns & H. 312.

For example, A contributes to B's periodical a dramatic or musical composition upon the terms that the copyright is to vest in B. This, as has been explained, gives B the right to publish the composition in the periodical, but does not give him the right to publish it as a separate publication without A's consent. Now suppose B or any other person publishes a separate edition of A's composition, A can sue without registration. But if anyone infringes B's copyright by publishing an unauthorised reprint of the complete periodical, then B must register prior to action.

We have next to consider the method of registration and the formalities to be observed.

The demand for entry in the Book of Registry must be addressed to the officer of the Stationers' Company, in the following form :—

I, A B, of ———, do hereby certify that I am the Proprietor of the Copyright of a Book entitled Y Z, and I hereby require you to make entry in the Register Book of the Stationers' Company of my Proprietorship of such Copyright, according to the particulars underwritten.

TITLE OF BOOK.	NAME OF PUBLISHER AND PLACE OF PUBLICATION.	NAME AND PLACE OF ABODE OF PROPRIETOR OF COPYRIGHT.	DATE OF FIRST PUBLICATION

Dated this ———— day of ————, 18 .

(Signed)   A B.

Witness: C D.

The entry itself must be as follows :—

TIME OF MAKING THE ENTRY.	TITLE OF BOOK.	NAME OF PUBLISHER AND PLACE OF PUBLICATION.	NAME AND PLACE OF ABODE OF PROPRIETOR OF COPYRIGHT.	DATE OF FIRST PUBLICATION.

Entry may be made at any time, provided it is made prior to action, just as a memorandum will satisfy section 4 of the Statute of Frauds, if made after the formation of the contract, but before action.

In Warne v. Lawrence it was held that "registration at Stationers' Hall, and subsequent issue of a writ in an action, although upon the same day, were a proper compliance with the provisions of the statute," and the injunction asked for was granted.

Per Kay, J. 24 W. R. 452.

Error as to any of the particulars in the above form of entry will, by force of section 24, prevent the proprietor of the copyright from suing, until rectified, and will also invalidate any subsequent assignment under section 13.

Low v. Routledge, 10 L.T.N.S. 838.

It would appear, however, from the case of Boosey v. Fairlie that irregularity as to registration is not always fatal. In that case the facts were as follows: "An opera entitled *Vert Vert* was composed by Offenbach and represented in France. By his permission, Soumis made two arrangements of the music, one for the piano and voice, and one for the piano alone. The opera was produced in Paris on March 10th, 1869, but never as a whole

7 Ch.D. 301.

printed. The two arrangements by Soumis were printed and published in Paris on March 28th, 1869. The music of the opera and the arrangements were assigned to Boosey. He registered them at Stationers' Hall, entering (correctly) March 10th as the date of first representation and March 28th as the date of first publication. This was true in fact as to the arrangement by Soumis, but not correct as to the opera itself, which at the time was still in manuscript. Boosey further entered himself as assignee of the copyright in the music of the said book and also the right of publicly performing such music. But the only copies deposited at Stationers' Hall were those of the arrangements by Soumis. The unpublished opera was never deposited. Fairlie produced a dramatic representation which he described as *Vert Vert*, music by Offenbach, taking the music from the arrangement by Soumis, the words being furnished by English librettists.

It was held that there had been a sufficient registration of the music of the opera to protect the plaintiff's copyright, although in fact the entries referred not to the original opera, but to Soumis' arrangement; and the ruling was affirmed on appeal.

<small>4 App. Cas. 711. Collingridge v. Emmott, W.N.(1887),216 Mathieson v. Harrod, L.R. 7 Eq., 272.</small>

The year, month, and day of the month must all be accurately set out. The year and month alone are insufficient.

The name of the first publisher must be given, and not merely that of the first publisher who registers, *e.g.*, A composes a song and sells copyright to B, who publishes but does not register it, since he knows it is time enough to register when the copyright has been infringed. B subsequently sells the copyright of the song to C, another publisher.

<small>Chappell v. Davidson, 18 C.B. 194. Weldon v. Dicks, 10 Ch.D. 252.</small>

During C's proprietorship the copyright is infringed. The necessity for registration has now occurred. In the entry, C must appear as proprietor, and B as publisher, although, in fact, C is the present publisher and B has ceased to publish the song.

This was held in a recent case (Coote *v.* Judd) following Weldon *v.* Dicks. "Registration of a copyright is bad if the name entered as that of 'the publisher' is not that of the first publisher."

23 Ch.D. 727.

"In my opinion," said Bacon, V.C., "the statute requires something more than registration of the name of the person who happens to be the publisher at the date of the registration; it requires that the name of the person who first published the book should appear, and this for the best of reasons, in order that everybody connected with the registration may ascertain for himself how far the right of a person claiming from or under the first publisher may be successfully challenged."

This case (Coote *v.* Judd) is instructive, as showing the necessity for care in registration where a composition has passed through various hands, and that a person may be a "publisher" within the meaning of an Act of Parliament who is not so in the business meaning of the term. The facts of the case were these:—

A commissioned B (a comic singer) to write a song, setting forth the merits of a commodity of which A was the manufacturer and sole proprietor. B appears to have been able to write the words and to sing the song, but he had to obtain the services of a nameless composer to provide the music. The song was in due course composed and sung. The three parties obtained what they bargained for. The nameless composer was paid for his music by B, though the fact did not transpire in the action; B was paid by A for his services as "Puff," and A had derived what benefit the puff produced. B, who had retained all rights over the composition, then sold it to D (the plaintiffs in the action). Subsequently E infringed D's rights. Registration then became necessary in order to enable D to sue. D appears to have entered himself as proprietor and publisher. The registration as "publisher" was held to be bad. B was the first publisher. "He who gets the song engraved and keeps the metal plates and lithographic stone" is the publisher. It is assumed that the learned judge (Baçon, V.C.) meant to convey that the person who holds the plates or lithographic stone has the control of the publication. It would seem, however, to be necessary to add some words as to issuing the composition to the public, for surely a mere order to an engraver to engrave plates and make copies therefrom, and the holding of those plates without issuing the composition engraved to the public, can hardly be held to constitute publication. Such a question after all is one of fact, and in the present case it was found as a fact that B did what amounted to publication, and that therefore he and not D should have entered as first publisher. Two similar cases suggest themselves. A dramatic author, instead of submitting a new play in manuscript, has it printed and kept on sale by Mr. S. French, the theatrical publisher, and submits it in that more acceptable form to a theatrical manager. If the copyright in the book is infringed, who is to be entered as publisher—the dramatic author, or French?

A composer, instead of submitting a song in manuscript to a singer or a publisher, has it engraved and holds the plates himself, but does not sell or attempt to sell any copies. Having eventually secured a singer to perform his song, he assigns his copyright to a person who is a "publisher" in the business sense of the term.

The copyright is subsequently infringed. Who is to be registered as first publisher?

If the definition as reported to have been given by the learned judge in Coote v. Judd is to be taken verbatim, the composer is the first publisher. But he has never issued copies of the song to the public, though it is true he has held the plates. It is submitted with some confidence that in the case quoted the further fact must have been found though not reported, or if not found ought to have been found in order to sustain the ruling, viz., that the person who "got the song engraved and kept the metal plates and lithographic stone," also sold copies or offered them for sale.

NAME OF PUBLISHER.

If the publisher be a firm, the trading name must be accurately entered. Thus if the members of a firm be Sampson Low, father and son, and Marston, but the trading name be Sampson Low & Co., the entry of Sampson Low and Marston is fatal.

Low & Routledge, 10 L.T.N.S. 838.

PLACE OF PUBLICATION.

Apparently, the place must be the place where the business of publication is carried on, and not the private residence of the publisher or publishers.

Nottage v. Jackson. 41 L.T.N.S. 339.

PERIODICALS.

In the case of periodicals or series of works, the date of publication must be that of the first number.

Dicks v. Yates, 18 Ch.D. 76.

EDITIONS.

Where new editions are published, which are merely reprints of the original, and the original has not been registered, registration, whenever it takes place, must show as date of publication the date of publication of the original edition. In the case of Thomas v. Turner three editions of the same work had been published, the two last being merely reprints of the first. The third edition only was registered, and the date of the publication of this was entered as the date of first publication. It was held, reversing the judgment of Bacon, V.C., that the plaintiff had not truly stated the time of first publication, within the meaning of s. 13 of 5 & 6 Vict., c. 45. "The

33 Ch.D. 292.

object of entering the date of first publication," said Lopes, L.J., " is no doubt to fix the time from which the forty-two years, the period of the duration of a copyright, are to run." But the learned judge went on to remark that " had the new edition been practically a new work, the result might have been different."

The matter is not unimportant in the case of musical compositions, where editions of the same work are numerous: and the discussion suggests the question: what constitutes an edition? According to Reade *v.* Bentley, an edition means "every quantity of books put forth to the bookselling trade and to the world at one time, and when the advertisements, the printing, and other well-known expenses and acts by a publisher bringing out such quantities in the ordinary way are closed, that constitutes the completion of the edition, whether the copies are taken from fixed or movable plates or types, or whether the types or plates are broken up or not, and whether all the copies taken are given forth and advertised for sale or retained and stored in the warehouse of the publisher." It is not so easy to determine what is an edition of a song or other musical composition. Probably in the case of a composition published on what is known as the "royalty" system, an edition would be held to consist of those copies which are signed by the composer or his agent in a batch, so to speak, since the signing is a condition precedent to the work being put forth upon the market, and the expense of production is temporarily closed.

27 L.J., Ch. 254.

DELIVERY OF COPIES.

A printed copy of the whole of every book and of all subsequent editions if containing additions or alterations, published in any part of the British dominions, must be delivered to the British Museum, the Bodleian Library at Oxford, the Public Library at Cambridge,

5 & 6 Vict., c. 45, s. 6.

the Library of the Faculty of Advocates at Edinburgh, and that of Trinity College, Dublin. 5 & 6 Vict., c. 45, s. 8.

The copy for the British Museum must be "bound, sewed, or stitched together, and printed upon the best paper on which the same shall be printed," and must be delivered within a month after publication if published in London, or within three months if elsewhere in the United Kingdom. The delivery may be made between 10 a.m. and 4 p.m. on any week-day, except Ash Wednesday, Good Friday, or Christmas Day. 5 & 6 Vict., c. 45, s. 6. — 5 & 6 Vict., c. 45, s. 7.

This delivery of "best copy" is a tax on publishers of books in the common meaning of the term; but it hardly affects musical or dramatic publications. Publishers of sheet music, however, must experience some annoyance in having to deliver their copies "stitched."

The delivery of copies to the other libraries mentioned differs in two points. A "best copy" is not required, nor need any copy be delivered unless and until demanded. Such demand must be "in writing, left at the place of abode of the publisher at any time within twelve months next after publication, under the hand of the officer of the Stationers' Hall," and copies must "be delivered within a month after demand to the officer of the said company for the use of the library for which the demand shall be made."

From this it would appear that if no demand is made by or on behalf of the libraries within the period specified, the obligation to deliver is discharged.

Any publisher may deliver copies at any of the said libraries, free of expense, to the librarians or other persons authorised; and "such delivery shall, to all intents and purposes of this Act, be held as equivalent to delivery to an officer of Stationers' Company." 5 & 6 Vict., c. 45, s. 9.

For default in delivering copies of any book or any

second or subsequent edition, the publisher "shall forfeit the value of the book or edition not delivered, and a sum not exceeding £5, to be recovered by the librarian of the library for the use of which such copy should have been delivered."

<small>5 & 6 Vict., c. 45, s. 10.</small>

Where a book consists of several volumes, the publishers are not liable for non-delivery of one volume.

<small>B. Museum v. Payne, 4 Bing. 548.</small>

Neglect to deliver copies differs in effect from neglect to register. Neglect to register precludes a proprietor from suing for infringement of his copyright. Neglect to deliver is no bar. Thus a defendant to proceedings for infringement may plead "non-registration," which is a complete plea until the defect is remedied. But "non-delivery of copies" is no plea to such proceedings.

<small>Low v. Routledge, 3 H.L. 100.</small>

INFRINGEMENT OF RIGHTS.

As before pointed out, the author or proprietor of a dramatic or musical composition has two kinds of rights :—

(a) The right of controlling the multiplication of copies, *i.e.*, copyright proper;
(b) The sole right of representation or performance, commonly called Acting or Performing Rights.

Each of these rights is infringed in a manner peculiar to itself.

(a) INFRINGEMENT OF COPYRIGHT PROPER.

Copyright is defined in the Interpretation clause of the Copyright Amendment Act to be "the sole and exclusive liberty of printing or otherwise multiplying copies." Infringement, therefore, occurs when any person, without consent of the proprietor, multiplies copies. On the principle that there is no right without a means of enforcing it, the law provides remedies

<small>5 & 6 Vict., c. 45.</small>

either by way of injunction or damages, according to the circumstances of the particular case. But in addition to this general infringement, with its general remedy, there are special forms of infringement of copyright set out in the Act, accompanied by special means of checking or obtaining redress for the same.

Section 15 provides that copyright is infringed if any person—

(1) In any part of the British Dominions prints, or causes to be printed, either for sale or exportation, any "book" in which there is subsisting copyright, without the consent, in writing, of the proprietor thereof;
(2) Imports for sale or hire any such "book," so having been unlawfully printed, from parts beyond the sea;
(3) Knowingly sells, publishes, or exposes to sale or hire, or causes to be sold, published, or exposed to sale or hire, or has in his possession for sale or hire any book so unlawfully printed or imported.

Two questions at once suggest themselves. First, what if the "book" be not printed, but written by hand or some process to which the term printing cannot apply? Secondly, what if the book be gratuitously circulated? It appears that no action would lie under this section. But the injured party is not on that account without his remedy. He can proceed in the ordinary course to enforce a right which has been conferred upon him by statute. He has the general rights and remedies conferred by the statute, although his case does not satisfy the requirements of this particular section. There is undoubted authority for this in the cases of Novello *v.* Sudlow and Warne *v.* Seebohn. In the former case music was copied without the consent of the proprietor of the copyright, and distributed *gratuitously* among the members of a musical society. It was held that this was a publication for which a party is liable as for an invasion

Novello *v.*
Sudlow,
12 C.B. 177.

39 Ch.D.
73.

of the property of the proprietor therein independently of section 15 of 5 & 6 Vict., c. 45. In Warne *v.* Seebohm the copies complained of were in *manuscript.*

Both these cases show that although to enable a person to sue under section 15 the copies must have been " printed " and " distributed for sale or hire," the proprietor, nevertheless, has a general remedy where the copies are not printed, and not distributed for sale or hire.

Besides the forms of piracy indicated in section 15 of the Copyright Amendment Act, the following are made penal offences by section 17 of the same Act :— *(5 & 6 Vict., c. 45, s. 17.)*

(1) If "any person, except the proprietor or some person authorised by him, import into any part of the United Kingdom or into any other part of the British Dominions for sale or hire any printed book first composed or printed and published in any part of the United Kingdom wherein there shall be copyright, and reprinted in any country or place whatsoever out of the British Dominions ; "

(2) " Import or bring, or cause to be imported or brought, for sale or hire, any such printed book into any part of the British Dominions ; "

(3) " Knowingly sell, publish, or expose to sale, or let to hire, or have in his possession for sale or hire any such book."

The following points seem to demand especial attention. By the terms of the section the offence consists in importing into British Dominions reprints of copyright works composed, and first printed and published, in the United Kingdom.

Again, section 17 is limited in terms to reprints made outside the British Dominions, while section 15 uses the phrase "parts beyond the sea." Does this mean outside the United Kingdom, or outside the British Dominions? If both sections as to this mean the same thing, there appears to be no provision made for the case of reprints made in one part of the British Dominions and imported into another. What is there in the statute to prevent the importation into England of an Australian reprint of an English composition? The matters are, however, now provided for by the Colonial Copyright Act.

It will also be observed that in both sections 15 and 17 there is a contrast between the offence of "importing for sale," and "selling" unauthorised copies. The latter to be within the Act must be done "knowingly." This was pointed out in the case of Cooper *v.* Whittingham, where it was held that ignorance of the nature of the imported copies could not be a defence where the offence charged was "importing for sale," but only where the offence charged was "selling knowingly."

<small>15 Ch. D. 501.</small>

Again, in the case of Leader *v.* Strange, in an action for infringement of copyright by merely publishing a work printed or caused to be printed by others, it was held that knowledge of the copyright so infringed must be proved. Therefore, where a proprietor of copyright intends to sue a person for selling knowingly, the better course is to give the importer notice that the copies imported are copyright.

<small>2 Car. & Kir. 1010.</small>

<small>Cooper *v.* Whittingham, 15 Ch. D. 501.</small>

(*b*) INFRINGEMENT OF PERFORMING-RIGHTS.

We have already seen in the preceding chapter what constitutes an unlawful performance of a dramatic composition. It is the representation of the whole or a part of a dramatic composition at a place of dramatic entertainment in any part of the British Dominions, without the written consent of the proprietor. Musical compositions are on a different footing.

Section 20 of the Copyright Amendment Act extends the provisions of the Dramatic Copyright Act to musical compositions, and section 21 of the same Act provides that the proprietor of the right of representing dramatic pieces or musical compositions shall have all the remedies given and provided in the 3 & 4 Wm. IV., c. 15. It will, however, be noticed by reference to the wording of the later Act, that whereas the Dramatic Copyright Act limits the unlawful representation to a "place of dramatic entertainment," the Copyright Amendment Act makes no mention of such a condition, nor is there any indication in the later statute as to how much of the earlier is incorporated. *(3 & 4 Wm. IV., c. 15. 5 & 6 Vict., c. 45, s. 20.)*

There is fortunately a judicial interpretation of the doubtful sections in the case of Wall v. Taylor. The plaintiff had the exclusive right of singing a song entitled the "Will o' the Wisp." The song was sung without the consent of the plaintiff at a concert, and at a place not used on any other occasion as a "place of dramatic entertainment." For the plaintiff it was said that the song was a "dramatic piece" within the meaning of 5 & 6 Vict., c. 45, and that it had been publicly performed or represented, and that therefore he was entitled to the penalty of 40s. On the other side it was argued that, assuming the song was one to the performance of which the plaintiff had an exclusive right, yet inasmuch as it was sung at a place which was not a "place of dramatic entertainment," the plaintiff was not entitled to recover any penalty, but only the amount of such damages as he thereby had suffered. *(11 Q.B.D. 102 C. A.)*

The question to be decided was whether section 21 of 5 & 6 Vict., c. 45, incorporates only the remedy given by section 2 of the Dramatic Copyright Act, or whether it also incorporates the condition or state of circumstances under which the right to remedy *(3 & 4 Wm. IV., c. 15.)*

arises, that is whether the unauthorised performance of a musical composition is unlawful, wherever it takes place, or only when at "a place of dramatic entertainment." The court (Cotton, L.J., dissenting) held that "the proprietor of the right of performance was entitled to the penalty given by section 2 of 3 & 4 Wm. IV., c. 15, even though the musical composition has not been represented at 'a place of dramatic entertainment.'"

Are we then to infer that in suing for an unlawful performance of a dramatic composition, the plaintiff need not show that it was performed at "a place of dramatic entertainment"? If so, the elaborate arguments in Duck *v.* Bates appear to be of no importance. Or, on the other hand, are we to infer that to constitute a wrong, the performance of musical compositions, when dramatic, must take place at a place of dramatic entertainment, while if not dramatic, such a condition is not necessary? According to this, an unauthorised performance of a song is unlawful if it takes place in a concert-room, while an unauthorised performance of an opera is not unlawful unless it be at a place of dramatic entertainment.

13 Q.B.D. 843 C.A.

Musical compositions differ from dramatic as to infringement in another respect.

By 45 & 46 Vict., c. 40, s. 1, it is provided that if the proprietor of the copyright in any musical composition or his assignee desires "to retain in his own hands exclusively the right of public representation or performance of the same," he must notify the same on the title-page.

Section 2 provides that if before publication the right of public representation or performance be vested in one person and the copyright (*i.e.*, the right to multiply copies) in another, and the former desires to retain the right of public representation or performance, he must give notice to the owner of the copyright requiring him to print upon every copy of such musical composition a notice that the right of public representation is reserved.

If, after publication, these two rights become separated and vested in different owners, then "if the owner of the right of public representation or performance shall desire to retain the same, he shall, before the publication of any further copies of the composition, give notice in writing to the owner of the copyright requiring him to print such notice as aforesaid on every copy of such musical composition to be thereafter published."

For non-compliance with such notice, the owner of the copyright shall pay to the owner of the right of public representation or performance the sum of £20, to be recovered in any court of competent jurisdiction.

An illustration will perhaps make the cases contemplated by the Act more clear.

A composes an opera, sells the copyright to B, but reserves the right of public performance.

Before publication A must require B to print upon the opera the notice that "the right of public performance is reserved." For default B is liable to pay A £20. This case falls within section 2.

Again, C composes an opera, sells copyright and right of public perormance to D. D publishes the work. Subsequently he sells to E the right of public performance. E must require D to print upon all subsequent copies the notice that "the right of public performance is reserved." For default D is liable as above. This case falls within section 3.

Section 4 effectually meets the case for which the Act was undoubtedly passed. It provides that, notwithstanding the provisions of the Dramatic Copyright Act, and the Copyright Amendment Act in which those provisions are incorporated, where the pro- *3 & 4 Wm. IV., c. 15. 5 & 6 Vict., c. 45.* prietor of the right of public performance of any musical composition published before the passing of the Act recovers no more than 40s. for an unauthorised performance, "the cost shall be in the discretion of the court or judge before whom the action is tried." A still further check upon vexatious proceedings is imposed by 51 & 52 Vict., c. 17, which provides that the court may award less than 40s.

It will be observed by reference to both these Acts (45 & 46 Vict., c. 40, and 51 & 52 Vict., c. 17), that it is only musical compositions that are provided for, there being no such discretion in the court as to damages and costs for the unauthorised performance of dramatic compositions.

LITERARY LARCENY.

So far we have been speaking of that kind of infringement which was described by James, L.J., in Dicks v. Yates as "open piracy." It occurs "where a publisher in this country publishes an unauthorised edition of a work in which copyright exists, or where a man introduces and sells a foreign reprint of such a work," or where an unauthorised representation or performance of a dramatic or musical composition is given. Its essence is that it is open. There is no concealment as to the authorship. A performs or publishes a work by B, announcing it to be by B, and he does it either as a piece of impudent appropriation, or in ignorance that it is a copyright work, or in the belief that he (A) has a right to use it.

18 Ch.D. 76.

The second mode is when a man pretending to be the author of a book illegitimately appropriates the fruit of a previous author's literary labour. This is "literary larceny," or as it is commonly called, plagiarism. Piracy does not consist in the quantity taken. "The quantity taken may be great or small, but if it comprises a material portion, it is

Per James, L.J., in Dicks v. Yates, 18 Ch.D. 76.

taken illegally. The question is as to the substance of the thing, and if there be no abstraction of that which may be substantially appreciated no penalty is incurred. . . . The question in every case must be a question of fact." *Per* Lord Hagan *in* Chatterton *v.* Cavo, 3 H.L. 493.

The American case of Daly *v.* Palmer illustrates what amounts to substantial identity. 6 Blatch. (Amer.) 256.

The same principle is laid down in Planché *v.* Braham. What degree of similarity will amount to a piracy, what is or is not a representation of part of a dramatic production, are questions of fact for a jury to determine. In that case the singing of two or three songs from plaintiff's libretto was held to be such a representation of part of a dramatic composition as amounted to a piracy. 4 Bing. N.C. 17.

In the case of musical compositions, piracy may be of part of a melody as well as of a whole. This was settled in D'Almaine *v.* Boosey. "It is a nice question what shall be deemed such a modification of an original work as shall absorb the merit of the original in the new composition. No doubt such a modification may be allowed in some cases as in that of an abridgment or digest . . . . but the subject of music is to be regarded on very different principles. It is the air or melody which is the invention of the author, and which may in such case be the subject of piracy, and you commit piracy if by taking not a single bar but several, you incorporate in the new work that in which the whole meritorious part of the invention consists. I remember in a case of copyright (the name would be interesting) at *nisi prius*, a question arising as to how many bars were necessary for the constitution of a subject or phrase. Sir G. Smart, who was a witness in the case, said a mere bar did not constitute a phrase, although three or four might do so. . . . But you might take the bars in different order or broken by the intersection of 1 Y. & C. 288.

F

others, like words (*sic*), in such a manner as should not be a piracy. It must depend on whether the air taken is substantially the same with the original. Now the most unlettered in music can distinguish one song from another, and the mere adaptation of the air, either by changing it to a dance, or by transposing it from one instrument to another, does not even to common apprehensions alter the original subject. . . . Substantially the piracy is where the appropriated music, though adapted to a different purpose from the original, may still be recognised by the ear."

Per **Lord Lyndhurst** *in* **D'Almaine v. Boosey.** 1 Y. & C. 288.

But neither the learned judge nor the musical expert has given us the benefit of opinion on the far more difficult question as to how far piracy of a musical composition is to be tested by "time" or rhythm on the one hand, or by notation on the other hand.

Suppose, for the sake of example, it is admitted that, as far as quantity is concerned, six bars of melody are sufficient if similar to constitute a piracy. In what is the similarity to consist? Is it in the fact that the notes are the same, or nearly the same, and arranged in the same, or nearly the same, sequence? But what of the "time"? Is the "time" to be regarded or not? Clearly if the notes are the same, and time is the same, then the melody is in every particular identical, and there is a piracy. But what if the notes are the same, and in the same sequence, but the time differs? It is perfectly possible that a melody may be reproduced note for note, and harmony for harmony, and yet by a skilful change of the time, there may be no similarity in sound. Let us suppose that A composes a melody, and that B takes the notes in their original sequence, but changes the time. Now, suppose A has secured copyright in his melody by performance or publication. Can he obtain an injunction or damages against B when the latter publishes what he calls "his" melody? It is conceived that A cannot do so. The essence of the wrong does not lie in the intention, however immoral, but in the damage caused. B, by an appropriation clearly dishonest in intention, has produced a musical composition which by some means he has disguised, so that in sound it is unlike A's. It cannot be "recognised by the ear"—the test mentioned in D'Almaine *v.* Boosey, and it would appear, therefore, that A is not injured in spite of B's appropriation. 1 Y. & C. 288.

Conversely, piracy may "be committed *bonâ fide.*" "It is enough that the publication complained of is in substance a copy." Suppose, therefore, in the above example B's melody is similar to A's in every respect, so that it produces on the ear a similar effect or impression, then it is a piracy, and A can restrain B, even if B has never seen or heard A's composition, and the similarity is merely what is termed a coincidence. Ignorance will not avail B, just as it will not in a patent case. *Per* Lord Ellenborough *in* Cary *v.* Kearsley. 4 Esp. 170.

If the foregoing inferences be correct, then a somewhat anomalous state of things is presented. A man may commit what the law regards as a piracy without ever having heard or seen the composition of which he is alleged to be the pirate.

As with music, so with dramatic compositions, "Piracy may be committed *bonâ fide,*" and may be of a part as well as of the whole. But the part must be a substantial one. It must really be a part and not a particle. Thus, in Chatterton *v.* Cave the importation of two scenes from A's drama into B's was held not to be the importation of a substantial part. On the other hand, in Planche *v.* Braham, the singing of two or three songs from plaintiff's libretto to an opera (Weber's *Oberon*) was found to be a representation of a "part," sufficient to constitute an 3 App. Cas. 483. 4 Bing. N.C. 17

infringement. From this it will be seen that each case must be treated on its merits. In each it is a question of fact, and it therefore seems needless in a work of this character to multiply illustrations.

REMEDIES FOR INFRINGEMENT.

We now come to the remedies for infringement. And here whether the wrong be what has been described as "open piracy," or whether it be "literary larceny," the remedies are the same.

(1) In the case of unpublished works, the author may recover damages in an action for any infringement by the unauthorised publication of his manuscripts or by the unlicensed representation or performance of his dramatic or musical compositions.

He has also a remedy by injunction to restrain the intended or continued doing of either of these acts, and an account of the profits made by the acts mentioned.

(2) In the case of published works, the proprietor of the copyright has at law and in equity the general remedies above mentioned, but he has, further, the following special remedies provided by statute.

REMEDY FOR PIRACY BY ACTION ON THE CASE.

5 & 6 Vict., c. 45.

Section 15 of the Copyright Amendment Act provides that for piracy, as defined on page 58, the remedy shall be by special action on the case. But special forms of actions being abolished, it would appear that the remedy is by ordinary action *in tort*. The piracy in this section mentioned consists of—

(1) Printing or causing to be printed in the British Dominions any copyright work for sale or exportation.
(2) Importing foreign reprints for sale or hire.

(3) Knowingly publishing, selling, or having in possession any book unlawfully printed or imported.

But it has been already pointed out that knowledge is essential in the last-mentioned offence.

Cooper v. Whittingham. 15 Ch.D.501.

SPECIAL PENALTY FOR UNLAWFUL IMPORTATION.

Besides the remedy by action for damages provided in section 15, there is a further check placed by the legislation upon unlawful importation. Section 17, which defines the offence, already explained on page 59, provides that—

(1) Every unlawfully imported "book" shall be forfeited, and shall be seized by any officer of Custom or Excise, and in that case must be destroyed by such officer.

(2) The offender shall upon conviction before two justices be fined £10 for every offence, and double the value of every copy of any such book in respect of which he commits such offence.

By section 23, a provision, which appears to be of great value as a protection for owners of copyright, is made to the effect that all copies of any book, in which there is copyright, unlawfully printed or imported without the consent in writing of the registered proprietor of the copyright, are to be deemed to be the property of the registered proprietor of such copyright, and he may sue for and recover the same with damages for the detention thereof from any person who detains them after a demand thereof in writing.

5 & 6 Vict., c. 45, s. 23.

Section 17 and section 23 appear at first sight to be in one respect irreconcilable. By the former it is enacted that unlawfully imported books shall be seized and destroyed by the officers of Custom or Excise, while section 23 gives to the injured proprietor the right to sue for and recover the copies, with damages from any person who detains them.

It may very well happen that the proprietor of copyright may desire to have possession of the forfeited copies. It may be advantageous, if he is a publisher, to him to put them into his own stock and sell them with or in lieu of his own printed copies. If he has this desire he must let it take practical shape speedily. His best course would be to notify the officers of the port where he has reason to expect an unlawful importation of his copyright works, and to request them to seize but not destroy the copies so unlawfully imported. If he do not take this course, and the officers of Customs or Excise be zealous officials, he may find to his disappointment ashes instead of books.

The Customs Consolidation Act (39 & 40 Vict., c. 36) goes further than the Act under consideration. The latter prohibits importation for sale or hire. The former prohibits importation simply. Thus to plead that the imported copies were imported for private use and not for sale or hire, would be a defence to proceedings under 5 & 6 Vict., c. 45, s. 17, but not under the Customs Act.

Again, the Copyright Amendment Act refers to works *5 & 6 Vict., c. 45.* first printed in the United Kingdom and printed or reprinted outside the British Dominions. Thus to import into the United Kingdom or any part of the British Dominions, copies made *in* the British Dominions, would appear to be no offence under this Act. *39 & 40 Vict., c. 36.* The Customs Act, however, prohibits the importation of works reprinted in any other country besides the United Kingdom; and therefore, importation into the United Kingdom from a British colony would be illegal. Further, by section 152 of the Customs Consolidation Act, importation to any part of the British Dominions is prohibited. This matter is dealt with in the chapter on Colonial Copyright. By the same Act, lists of copyright works are to be publicly exposed at the Custom Houses in the several ports of the United Kingdom. Notice is to be given in writing to the Commissioners of Customs of the date of expiration of the copyright in such works; and by section 45, wrongful entry in such lists may be expunged by order of a judge in chambers.

REMEDY BY INJUNCTION.

So far we have dealt with remedies by action for damages and penalties. There is also a remedy by injunction to restrain the commission or continuance of any act of infringement. And it is open to the injured party to avail himself of this remedy, as well as or instead of the remedies provided by the statutes. If there were any doubt as to this, it may be regarded as dispelled by the ruling in Cooper v. Whittingham. "Where a statute creates a new offence and imposes a penalty, the auxiliary remedy may still be claimed." [15 Ch.D. 501.]

CHAPTER III.

INTERNATIONAL COPYRIGHT.

INTRODUCTORY REMARKS.

THE branch of our subject indicated by the above heading is purely the creature of statute. Our judges have never recognised any inherent right, either in a British subject or an alien, to exclude others from multiplying copies of or publicly representing works first published beyond the territorial limits.[1] Increased facilities of communication, both physical and mental, have made it necessary to abolish this state of things as an anachronism; and a statute was passed in the year 1844,[2] which is the basis of all the present law bearing on international rights in musical and dramatic works.

[1] Guichard v. Mori 9, L.J., Chy., 227.
[2] The International Copyright Act, 1844.

A statute already in existence (which was known as "The International Copyright Act,"[3] purported to create copyright available for Great Britain with reference to literary works first published in a foreign country; but until the International Copyright Act, 1844, no attempt was made to create reciprocal rights between Great Britain and friendly nations in reference specifically to dramatic and musical works.

[3] 1 & 2 Vict., c. 59.

According to a recital in the International Copyright Act, 1844, the previous law had been found insufficient to confer upon authors of books first published abroad copyright analogous to that conferred by the Copyright Amendment Act with reference to books first published here,

By the enacting part of the International Copyright Act, 1844,[1] power is given to the Queen to direct by an Order in Council that as respects books which shall after a future time to be specified in such order, be first published in any foreign country to be named in such order, the authors shall have copyright during such period as shall be defined in such order, not exceeding the term to which authors of the like works published here may be entitled.

[1] 7 Vict., c. 12.

By section 3, all and singular the enactments of the Copyright Amendment Act are to apply to books to which the Order in Council shall extend.

By the same statute, section 5,[2] an Order in Council may direct that the authors of dramatic pieces and musical compositions, first publicly represented or performed abroad, shall have the sole liberty of representing or performing here such pieces or compositions during such period as shall be defined in the order; and from and after such time the enactments of the Copyright Amendment Act (*inter alia*) shall apply to those works to which the order shall extend, and which shall have been registered as if such pieces and compositions had been first publicly represented and performed here.

[2] 7 Vict., c. 12, s. 5.

TREATIES WITH FOREIGN COUNTRIES.

Under the powers of the International Copyright Act, 1844, and Orders in Council based upon it, treaties were from time to time entered into between Great Britain and the following countries:—

13th May, 1846	Prussia.
24th August, 1846	Saxony.
30th March, 1847	Brunswick.
1st July, 1847	Thuringian Union.
4th August, 1847	Hanover.
28th December, 1847	Oldenburg.

3rd November, 1851	France.
8th February, 1853	Anhalt.
16th August, 1853	Hamburg.
12th August, 1854	Belgium.
14th June, 1855	Prussia, Supplementary.
7th July, 1857	Spain.
30th November, 1860	Sardinia.

THE BERNE CONVENTION.

The general purport of the treaties in question was to give the authors of works first published in one of the Federated States the same privileges in the other States as would be enjoyed if the work had been published there. Stringent registration clauses were added. By an Order in Council, dated the 28th November, 1887, the previous orders on which the treaties in question were founded, have been revoked with a view to consolidating the procedure in a convention founded on a conference held at Berne in 1885. A draft treaty was then prepared for giving to authors of literary and artistic works, first published in one of the federated countries, copyright in such works throughout the other countries parties to the convention. Those countries are:—

Great Britain,	Germany,	Belgium,
Spain,	France,	Haiti,
Italy,	Switzerland,	Tunis.

The Order in Council empowering Great Britain to enter into the Berne Treaty was made under the provisions above stated of the International Copyright Act, 1844,[1] supplemented by the International Copyright Act, 1886.[2]

[1] 7 Vict., c. 12.
[2] 49 & 50 Vict., c. 33.

By the later Act it was recited that the draft convention had been agreed to, and it is provided that the Act of 1886 and the previous International Copyright Acts shall be construed together; and then occur executory provisions which are practically repeated in a subsequent Order in Council, and in the Berne Treaty itself. There are, however, also other provisions, which do not cover entirely the same ground as any clause in the order or treaty.

Power is given[1] to Her Majesty to make Orders in Council for the purposes of the earlier International Copyright Acts, as well as of the now stating one, for revoking or altering any Order in Council previously made.[2] But any order so to be made is not to affect any rights acquired or accrued at the date of such order coming into operation, and shall provide for the protection of such rights.

[1] Sect. 10, sub-sect. 1.
[2] Sect. 10, sub-sect. 2.

By an Order in Council coming into operation on the 6th December, 1887, made under the International Copyright Acts, 1844 to 1886, effect is given to the Berne Treaty, which, translated into English, is appended to the order. The International Copyright Act, 1886, is also incorporated with the order.

Section 3 provides that the author of a work first produced in one of the countries of the Union shall have "the same right of copyright" (*sic*) including rights of representation, as if the work had been first produced here, and for the same period.

Order 23, Nov., 1887, Sect. 3.

It will be seen that the provision neither follows the terms of the similar clause in the Act of 1844, nor does it exactly correspond with the cognate clause in the convention itself. The Order in Council confers "the same right of copyright" (whatever that may mean), as if the work had been produced here, while the convention, as will be afterwards seen, confers *the same rights as the law grants to natives.* The Act of 1844 had granted copyright simpliciter. One is tempted to ask, on finding this divergence, whether the three forms are intended to import the same thing; and if so, why the provisions have been repeated, or at all events why different language has been used; if, on the other hand, a different import is contemplated, it ought to have been clearly shown in what the difference lies.

Again, we find some provisions, but not all, of the convention repeated in the Order in Council without any apparent reason. Why, for instance, should the provision to the effect that in the case of simultaneous production in two countries, the first production shall be taken to have been in the country where the term of copyright is shortest, be set out substantively in the Order in Council, while referential insertion is thought sufficient for the not less important provision that translations are to be entitled to protection as original works?

The Berne Treaty itself was ratified on the 5th Sept., 1887, and is provided to take effect from the expiration of three months after the exchange of the ratifications (it is presumed that calendar months are referred to).

The treaty is to operate until notice of withdrawal shall have been given by one of the parties, and will then remain in full force as regards the other parties.

The scope of the treaty was by separate document ("procés verbal de signature") declared to comprehend the United Kingdom of Great Britain and Ireland and all the Colonies and remote possessions ("possessions étrangères") of Her Britannic Majesty. Power of giving a substantive notice of withdrawal was reserved to Great Britain in respect of India, Canada, Newfoundland, the Cape, Natal, New South Wales, Victoria, Queensland, Tasmania, South Australia, Western Australia, and New Zealand.

[1]Berne Treaty, Art. 15. Power is reserved to the several Governments to make mutual arrangements extending the rights given by the treaty; not to be contrary, however, to anything originally contained in it.

An international office is constituted to be situated

in Switzerland. Article 17 contemplates revision, and improvements to be determined upon in future conference. The first conference is to take place at Paris at an interval of from four to six years from the date of the treaty coming into operation. *Art. 16, 17.*

The treaty unites the nations whose representatives have signed it into a confederated body for the protection of authors' rights. *Berne, Treaty, Art. 1.*

The interpretation clause adopts as a generic term "literary and artistic works," and defines it as comprising among other items "dramatic and dramatico-musical works," a definition which will not be thought an unnecessary truism by those who remember how many dramatic works are produced yearly which would not without some such clause be pronounced either "literary" or "artistic." Musical compositions, whether settings of words or not, are also comprised under the same term. By an instrument called "Protocole de Clôture," separately executed by the signatories, ballets and ballet-pantomimes were comprised under the head of "Œuvres dramatico-musicales;" and itinerant grinders of street organs and "pianos mécaniques" are relieved from the fear of finding themselves defendants to an action by an article in the last-mentioned protocol, which humanely declares that the sale of instruments reproducing melodies by mechanical device shall not be deemed an infringement of authors' rights.

The joint effect of the International Copyright Acts, 1844 and 1886,¹ Order in Council, and convention is to confer upon authors belonging to the confederated countries, or the representatives of those authors, rights in each of the other countries similar to those which natives of each of the countries in question would enjoy at home for works falling within one of the two following classes, viz.:— *7 Vict.c.12, s. 2, 49 & 50 Vict.,c. 33*

(1) Works published in a country of the union;

(2) Works not published at all.

The term of protection is limited so as not to exceed that of "the country of origin;" which phrase is defined by article 2 to be the country where publication has first occurred.

The provision as to duration is an echo of an enactment in the International Copyright Act, 1886. The article in the Convention which confers the rights in question is calculated to excite the admiration of the strictest purists, the words allotting the several rights to the several nationalities being a triumph of distributive grammar. The expression "Les auteurs ressortissant a l'un des pays de l'Union" is a pregnant one, feebly rendered in the English translation appended to the treaty by the words "authors of any country of the Union": the term "ressortissant" is no doubt not easily convertible; it implies, not merely that the subject of it is French, English, or German in a popular sense, but points to technical rights and liabilities of nationality.

The same article [1] also provides that the accomplishment of the conditions and formalities prescribed by law in the country *where the work took its origin* is to be a condition precedent to the enjoyment of protection under the treaty—that as to published works the country of first publication shall be the country of origin of the work; and that as to unpublished works, the country to which the author belongs is to be taken as that where the work first saw the light.

[1] Berne Convention, Art. 2.

The large scope of article 2 will, in cases regulated by the treaty, close the door to any such question as was raised in Boucicault v. Delafield with reference to the nationality of the plaintiff.[2] In the original French of that branch of article 2 which provides that as to unpublished works, the country of origin of the work is to be *that to which the author belongs*, the

[2] 1 Hem. & Mil. 597.

vigorous expression above referred to as descriptive of the nationality of the author ("ressortissant a l'un des pays de l'Union") does not recur, but though the language is different the import must be taken to be identical.

The provisions of article 2 are by article 9 extended to public performance of dramatic works and the lyric drama, whether the works in question have or have not been published ("que ses œuvres soient publiées ou non"). Article 2 is also made to apply to musical pieces, whether published or not, but subject to an obligation on the author to state on the title or at the commencement of the piece that he forbids public performance.

<small>Berne Convention, Art. 9.</small>

The subdivision into the drama, the lyric drama, and music is new, and speaks for itself.

The enactment in this article relating to translations is reserved for the section which treats of that subject generally.

Article 2 provides that in case of simultaneous publication in two of the federated countries of the Union, the country in which the term of protection is shortest shall be taken to be the country of origin of the work.

It is not easy to conceive how a case of literally simultaneous publication in two countries can arise in practice, and the difficulty of applying the clause must often be considerable; but the possibility of such a case is foreshadowed by section 3 of the International Copyright Act, 1886, and has been mooted[1] in some of the earlier authorities.[2] No such suggestion is to be found in the International Copyright Act, 1844.

<small>[1] Cocks & Purday, 2; Car. & Kir., 269.
[2] Routledge v. Low, L.R. 3 H.L. 100.</small>

It is not always easy to assign a date to publication, especially in the case of a work published abroad by exposure for sale, where the person interested in ascertaining the date is not on the spot; and one of the writers was compelled to abandon registration in Great Britain of a musical composition published in Germany by exposure for sale, because it could not be ascertained with accuracy at what precise date the work in question had been actually exposed in the publisher's window. The difficulty of identifying simultaneous publication must be far greater. If the publication consisted in public representation, would the question of date turn upon the fact that in one country the play or opera was performed at a matinée, in the other at night? There is nothing in the Convention or the Act authorising a tribunal to treat a day as indivisible.* The burden of proving the precise date would be upon the person suing, and it would very frequently happen that an action would fail from the difficulty of obtaining evidence of such date. The importance of the doctrine, however, is obvious. Suppose an action brought at the expiration of forty-five years or thereabouts from publication on a book believed to have been simultaneously published in London and Paris. If that belief is found to be correct, the time of copyright in France would be that of Great Britain, where the period is shortest, and the plaintiff would fail; but if it turned out that the first publication was French the plaintiff would be entitled to recover, as the term of forty-five years would not have exhausted the author's right in the country of origin of the work.

The Convention does not in express terms specify the period for which international copyright is to exist; but it does so referentially by giving to every author of any country of the Union the rights in the other federated countries which the respective laws of such countries grant to natives.

---

* As to splitting up a day see Warne v. Laurence, 34 W.R. 452, 30 Sol., J., in which Mr. Justice Kay decided that an entry on the register, made at half-past one, was sufficient to support a writ issued at a later period in the same day. See also Gartside v. Silkstone Co., 21 Ch.D. 767.

In Great Britain such rights are the author's life and seven years, or forty-two years from the first publication, whichever is the longest.

An Englishman first publishing here gets in each of the countries of the Union whatever rights such country grants to its natives, and for the same term. The period of protection, however, in any country cannot be greater than the term allowed in the country of origin.

THE RETROSPECTIVE OPERATION OF THE RECENT ENACTMENTS.

The retrospective operation of the present law depends upon three enactments, viz. :

(1) Section 6 of the Act of 1886.
(2) Section 3 of the Order in Council of December, 1887.
(3) Article 14 of the Berne Convention as modified by article 4 of the "Protocole de Clôture."

Section 6 of the International Copyright Act, 1886, invites litigation to an extent which deserves the gratitude of lawyers (if any such there be) who look on their calling less as an end than a means. The enactment provides that where an order is made with reference to any foreign country, the author and publisher of any work first produced before the order operates shall be entitled to the same rights and remedies as if the Acts and order had applied to the foreign countries at the date of the production. *(49 & 50 Vict., c. 33, s. 6.)*

The Order in Council of November 28th, 1887 (in the style familiar to us in connection with such documents) contains a clause purporting to cover the same ground as section 6, and being apparently surplusage.

The orders under which the hereinbefore referred to treaties took their rise are revoked ; and then follows a saving clause which is hereinafter commented on.

The cognate clause in the Berne Treaty is article 14, which limits the scope of the Convention to all works which at the moment of its coming into force have not yet fallen into the public domain in their country of origin. The operation of article 14 is subject to a reserve of any conditions which may be afterwards determined by agreement between all the parties; and this is followed up by a clause in the "Protocole de Clôture"[1] to the effect that in applying the treaty to the works in question, any stipulations contained in any existing or future treaties, and having a bearing on the subject, are to have due effect; and if there are no such stipulations, each country of the Union may settle the matter by domestic legislation.

[1] Protocole, Art. 4.

This latter clause may for present purposes be disregarded as far as Great Britain is concerned, for the orders on which the former conventions with the federated countries were founded are revoked; and there has been no subsequent legislation.

Section 6 in the Act of 1886 would seem not to be coextensive with the Berne Treaty, having no operation with reference to a dramatic or lyric piece in manuscript which has not been publicly performed, but which might call for protection under some circumstances; as, for instance, if the manuscript were surreptitiously obtained from the author's desk.

But the main question which arises upon this difficult section[2] of the Act of Parliament in combination with the order and treaty is what is its retrospective limit.

[2] Sect. 6.

There is more than one possible construction. It has been generally assumed that section 6 applied to all works, however ancient, which would have been entitled to protection had they been published here, even in cases where, owing to neglect to register, the foreign author would, but for the section, have lost the privilege given him by the

International Copyright Acts, and this being so, the proviso which is annexed to it assumes great importance. That proviso enacts, that where any person has before the publication of an Order in Council "lawfully produced any work in the United Kingdom," nothing in the section shall diminish or prejudice any rights or interests arising from or in connection with such production, which are subsisting and valuable when the order is published.

In connection with this clause must be considered the clause in the order of 1887, and which is there appended as a qualification to the clause revoking the previous orders on which the earlier conventions were founded. This clause and the proviso contained in section 6 obviously cover much of the same ground. The former runs as follows:—

> "Neither such revocation nor anything else in this order shall prejudicially affect any right acquired or accrued before the commencement of this order, by virtue of any order hereby revoked, and any person entitled to such right shall continue entitled thereto, and to the remedies for the same in like manner as if this order had not been made."

Both provisoes are of equal authority, the order in Council being made under the sanction of a statute.[1] In cases falling within both, it may be a question which is to prevail.

[1] 49 & 50 Vict., c. 33, s. 10.

These clauses have received an official interpretation in

the case of Moul *v.* Groenings. The defendant, a bandmaster at Brighton, had purchased of an English publisher, named Lafleur, for 2s. 6d., the score of a French piece of music which had been allowed to become public property by neglect to register under the Convention with France of 1851 ; the defendant had, after such purchase, rehearsed and publicly performed the piece before the coming into operation of the Order in Council of 1887. Proceedings were taken by the French Société des Auteurs, represented by Mr. Moul, claiming an injunction and damages, in respect of performances continued after the order came into operation. No evidence was given bearing on the question of the value to the defendant of the performing right, other than proof of the purchase, rehearsal, and performance. The Divisional Court, and afterwards the Court of Appeal, held that the defendant had acquired an interest in the piece within the meaning of the proviso, and that it must be assumed that such interest was valuable. The Court went upon two grounds : (1) that the bandmaster had himself a substantive interest independently of Lafleur ; and (2) that Lafleur, who had incurred expense in printing a work at a time when he could lawfully produce it, had also an interest which would have been prejudiced and rendered valueless if executants were to be restrained from performance. The observations of Lord Justice Lindley, however, laid great stress upon the professional character of the defendant. " How could we judicially say " (said his Lordship more than once in the course of the argument) "that this man, who gets his living

1891 2. Queen's Bench Division, Law Reports, 443.

by performing pieces of music, has no interest in a work which he has purchased in the course of business." It would seem that an amateur who had before the 6th December, 1887, for the amusement of friends, or for the benefit of a charity, performed a piece of music first published in one of the countries signatories to the Berne Convention, would not be exempted by the doctrine of Moul *v.* Groenings from the liability to penalties in respect of performance after that date, unless he could shelter himself under some publisher who had produced the work in England, as Lafleur did. Nor would it seem that mere performance, without the expenditure of a sum of money or money's worth in time and trouble, would confer a "valuable interest" even on a professional artist.

On the other hand, it would seem that individual members of the band, who had not actually performed the piece sought to be protected before the 6th December, 1887, would nevertheless be exempted from penal consequences, as the plaintiff could not reach them without by the same stroke prejudicing both the interests of the publisher, and of their employer, the bandmaster. It is perhaps unnecessary to remark that the publisher himself would be entitled to sell off all printed copies, and use type set up and stereotype plates. This was not only assumed, but stated by the learned judges who decided this important case.

As all the judges in the Divisional Court as well as in the Appeal Court were clearly of opinion that even if the plaintiff was right in other respects, the defendant was protected by the proviso, it became unnecessary to decide whether some and what registration was not a necessary condition prior to suing. This point would affect all actions brought by virtue of the Berne Convention, irrespective of its retroactive operation, but it will nevertheless be convenient to point out in this place how the matter stands as to registration, the question having been argued though not decided in Moul *v.* Groenings.

The provision in the statute of 1886 which relates to registration is contained in section 4, which enacts that "where an order respecting any foreign country is made under the International Copyright Acts, the provisions of those Acts with respect to the registry and delivery of copies of works shall not apply to works produced in this country, except so far as provided by the order."

A question then arises whether a foreigner coming here to sue as a member of one of the federated countries is exempted by section 4 from any registration at all. It has been recently held by a very able judge, that registration in the manner prescribed by the Copyright Acts is still a condition precedent to suing, and that the phrase "International Copyright Acts" is to be read as importing only the statutes strictly answering that description, to the exclusion of all others. This is important, as the registration forms are not the same under the *International Copyright Acts* as under the *Copyright Acts* properly so called, which latter Acts

Fishburn v. Hollingshead, 1891, 2 Ch. 371.

require entry of the name and abode of the publisher, particulars not necessary under the International Copyright Acts. (See Appendix vi.)

WHAT AMOUNTS TO PUBLICATION?

The case of Boucicault *v.* Delafield decides, as has been seen, the neat point that representation of a dramatic work amounts to publication. This doctrine is still of importance.

The Convention of Berne does not contain any precise statement that representation is to have the effect of publication. It is true that article 9 applies the stipulations of article 2 to the public performance of dramatic or dramatico-musical works, "whether such works are published or not" ("*que ces œuvres soient publiées ou non*"), but this would only seem to be intended to assimilate right of performance to right of multiplying copies, and not to affirm the proposition that every public representation of a play, every performance of a musical composition, involves its "publication" in the technical sense. The doctrine of Boucicault *v.* Delafield is therefore still of importance even as regards the federated countries, in a case, for instance, arising under the 3rd article of the treaty, which provides that the Convention shall apply to publishers of literary or artistic works "published" in one of the federated countries, in cases where the author is a subject of a country outside the federation. Suppose Messrs. Brandus, the French publishers, sue in England in respect of an alleged infringement of copyright by printing the opera first performed in Paris, *but not otherwise published*, of a Russian subject. But for Boucicault *v.* Delafield it might be a good defence that the work had not been "published" within the meaning of article 3.

An important provision in the statute of 1844 enacts that

"neither the author of any book, nor the author or composer of any dramatic piece or musical composition," first published abroad, is to have any copyright or exclusive right of public representation or performance other than such, if any, as he may become entitled to under the Act.

<small>International Copyright Act, 1844, sect. 19.</small>

In the case of Boucicault *v.* Delafield the plaintiff had for the first time represented the play of the *Colleen Bawn* in New York, with which state no international copyright treaty has ever existed, and he sued the defendant for infringement of an alleged right of representation by performance in England. It was argued for the plaintiff that there was an inherent common law right to restrain representations of an unpublished piece, and that a representation on the stage was not publication for purposes of copyright. It was argued for the plaintiff that the case of Donaldson *v.* Beckett applied, in which there was a difference of opinion between the judges as to the existence of a common law right, and whether, if it had existed, it had been taken away by statute. It was also argued for the plaintiff that the usage of the word "author" in section 19 must be restricted to an author being a subject of a country with which there is international copyright. It appeared that the work had been printed, but no stress was laid upon this fact in the judgment.

<small>1 H. & M. 597.</small>

<small>2 Bro., P.C. 129.</small>

<small>8 Ann. c. 19.</small>

The Vice-Chancellor held that, assuming that either under the common law, or the earlier statutes, the plaintiff might be entitled to some rights, the 19th section of the International Copyright Act, 1844, had annihilated them, and that it made no difference that the plaintiff could not have gained a title by registration, inasmuch as there was no convention with America. The learned judge declined to accede to the argument that the object of the Act in question was merely to extend, under certain conditions, to foreigners publishing their compositions abroad, rights which had previously belonged to British subjects; and that it could not be the object of the 19th section to take away from British subjects rights which they already enjoyed. "The generality of the 19th clause" was too great to admit of qualification. The learned judge seemed to consider that the statute was intended to hold out a sort of premium to British subjects to give the first representation of their works at home. In effect, the statute says, continues the judgment, that if after the passing of this Act a British subject or other person chooses to deprive this country of the advantage of the first publication of a new work, then he may have whatever benefits he may be entitled to under the statute; but that if he chooses to publish first in a country which has not availed itself of the privileges conferred by the Act, he shall be excluded from the benefits which he otherwise might have claimed. With great deference to the eminent judge who decided the case, there is nothing in the statute to point to any such penalty for depriving this country of the advantage in question, and it is far more probable, and more in accordance with the mode in which the Act is otherwise framed, to suppose that the combination of circumstances in Boucicault *v.* Delafield, viz., the case of a British subject publishing in a country not in treaty with England, never occurred to the draftsman. Moreover, it is noteworthy that the statute does not make first publication *by the author* necessary, but the fact of publication alone, by whomsoever done, will entitle the author to copyright. Therefore, if Mr. Boucicault's piece had been surreptitiously obtained, and first published in England (by no means an unprecedented case), such publication, which would not have been due to any meritorious desire on the part of the author to give this country the first-fruits of his talent, would, nevertheless, have enabled him to claim the privileges of copyright, a result which would seem to go far to negative the Vice-Chancellor's theory of privileges held out as a reward.

In a case where the same plaintiff claimed an injunction to restrain the defendant from representing a dramatic performance called *The Shaughraun*, which had been composed by the plaintiff and first performed in New York; the play had not been printed, and it was sought to distinguish the case from that last cited on that ground. It was argued that representation was not publication within the meaning of section 19, but the Court held the contrary, and that the case was undistinguishable from Boucicault *v.* Delafield.

<small>Boucicault *v.* Chatterton, 5 Ch. Div. 267.</small>

<small>1 H. & M. 597.</small>

James, L.J., expressed himself with the unhesitating conviction which usually characterised the utterances of that eminent judge. Baggallay, L.J., concurred, but in a judgment the force of which is qualified by doubts which are not easy to comprehend. It would seem that such light clouds would have been at once dispelled by the short argument (which does not seem to have occurred to those engaged in the case) that if a first representation is not equivalent to publication, there can be no exclusive right of performance at all under the Act in a manuscript dramatic work; the section which confers exclusive right of performance only applies to works already published, and no other practical or reasonable means of publication of a manuscript play than some form of representation can be conceived. The statute therefore must have contemplated publication by means of representation, unless it be sought to deny the possibility of exclusive right of representation in connection with a manuscript, which was not suggested in the case.

<small>Section 2, International Copyright Act, 1844.</small>

TRANSLATIONS OF WORKS THE SUBJECT OF INTERNATIONAL COPYRIGHT.

By the International Copyright Act, 1886 (which, as will be remembered, refers to the draft Convention of Berne), it is enacted[1] that where a work is first produced in a federated country, the author shall have the same right of preventing the production in and importation into the United Kingdom of any translation as he has with reference to the original work; but if after ten years[2] from the production of the original work, an authorised translation in English has not been produced, such right shall cease.

[1] Sec. 5, sub-sect. 1.
[2] Sub-sect. 2.

The law of copyright[3] is to apply to lawfully produced translations as if they were original works.

[3] Sub-sect. 3.

By the interpretation clause "production" is made to include "representation," if the case requires.

By the Berne Treaty[4] authors, members of one of the federated states, are to enjoy in the others the exclusive right of making or authorising the translation of their works ("droit exclusif de faire ou autoriser la traduction de leurs ouvrages") till the expiration of ten years from the publication of the original work in one of the federated states.

[4] Berne Treaty, Art. 5.

The 31st December of the year in which the original work was published is taken as the date of publication for the purposes of ascertaining the duration of exclusive right.

By the following article[5] lawful translations are to be protected as original works, and to have protection under articles 2 and 3 from reproduction in the federated states. In the case of a work of which the right of translation is public property ("dans le domaine public") the translator cannot restrain another translation by a different hand.

[5] Art. 6.

By article 9 the stipulations of article 2 are applied to public performances on the stage, whether spoken or lyric, and whether published or the reverse. ("Aux œuvres dramatiques ou dramatico-musicales, que ces œuvres soient publiées ou non.")

<small>Art.9, Berne Treaty.</small>

By article 9 also authors of plays and operas are, as long as their exclusive right of translation endures ("pendant la durée de leur droit exclusif de traduction"), protected against unlicensed public performance of translation of their works.

<small>Art.9, Berne Treaty.</small>

We have seen that by the Act of 1886[1] the author, *unless the treaty otherwise directs*, shall have the power of preventing the production of an unauthorised translation for the full term of copyright.

<small>[1] Sect. 5, Sub-sect 1.</small>

The treaty has, operating under the words in italics, cut down this right to the decennial period; and thus rendered inoperative the provision as to an English translation, which provision has accordingly been omitted from the treaty.[2] Though now in abeyance, however, the enactment may be resuscitated by some future Order in Council authorising a treaty under which the exclusive right of translation might be conferred for the full term of copyright.

<small>[2] Art. 5 & 6.</small>

"Produce" is defined by the interpretation clause,[3] to mean "published or made" or "performed or represented" as the occasion requires. In section 5, the word is so used as to bring both meanings into play.

<small>[3] 49 & 50 Vict., c. 33, s. 11.</small>

The phrase "author or publisher" under section 5 takes in the case of the former belonging to one of the federated countries (in which case the rights are vested in him personally); and the alternative position of the author being an outsider,[4] in which case the treaty substitutes the publisher for him.

<small>[4] Berne Treaty, Art. 3.</small>

In the English version of the treaty, the expression

"traductions licites" in article 6 is rendered "authorised translations," a version not very correct, and singularly infelicitous; as it appears to refer to the power conferred a few lines before upon authors of "authorising" translations; whereas the phrase is intended to comprise the case of a translation lawfully made through the right having become public property.

As to the right of performance applied to translations of works published abroad, "production" in section 5 of the statute[1] includes "representation," therefore the exclusive right of representation is assimilated for all purposes (including duration) by the Act of Parliament to copyright. By the treaty, however,[2] in the case of translation the author's exclusive right is limited to ten years, and by article 9, the exclusive right of representation of the translated work is made to correspond in this respect: "*pendant la durée de leur droit exclusif de traduction les œuvres sont réciproquement protégées contre la représentation publique.*" Every independent translation, however (by which is meant a version taken from the fountain head, and not from the work of some previous translator), is both by the Act of 1886 and the treaty to be deemed an original work; and as such entitled under article 2[3] to the same length of protective right as a native of the country of the forum for the time being would have. The last gap in an elegant mosaic is then filled in by article 9, which extends the provisions of article 2, including duration of right, to works destined for the histrionic and lyric stage. The whole of this portion of the treaty is couched in language of a terse neatness of which the French tongue is alone capable. It cannot be too clearly borne in mind that there is a broad line of demarcation between the mere infringement of the author's right of restraining any unauthorised translation made by an independent translator

[1] 49 & 50 Vict., c. 33, s. 5.
[2] Berne Treaty, Art. 2.
[3] Berne Treaty, Art. 2.

(a right which only lasts for ten years) on the one hand; and on the other, the act of a thief, who reaps in the field of a previous translator by stealing a version which may perhaps show as much literary ability as was involved in the creation of the original work.

To sum up, the joint operation of the statutory and conventional clauses as to translations is as follows: during the ten year period the author may, by himself or his appointee, make a translation in any language of his work, and may restrain any one else from issuing, vending, or representing without licence from him either that version or any other. After the expiration of that period, the author or any other translator may restrain during the whole period of copyright under article 2, the issue, sale, or performance of an actual or colourable copy of any version which such author or translator may have made. The author's right of interfering with independent translators will, however, have ceased.

To apply the provisions of the articles 5, 6 and 9 to living subject matter, let us shift the date of the facts relating to the production of Wagner's opera *Rienzi*, a work which was first given in France. We have an author belonging to Germany, a country of the Union, producing a lyric drama in another of the federated states. The great composer wrote his own libretto, and in the present case the text was published by circulation in the theatre, concurrently with performance. Let us also assume that he employed an Italian to translate the libretto direct from the German for production at Covent Garden, and that a rival manager wishing to give the opera at Her Majesty's Theatre reprints the Italian translation made by order of the composer. The libretto is registered with all proper formalities in France, that being all that is necessary. Another rival manager employs Mr. Sutherland Edwards to turn into English the German libretto for the purpose of public performance as a play by a touring company in Dublin, the language undergoing some necessary modification for the purpose of declamation in lieu of singing.

We have thus most of the combinations likely to occur in practice. Herr Wagner could obtain from the English tribunal an injunction to restrain,

(1) The manager of Her Majesty's Theatre, and his artists from performing,

(2) The same manager and his servants from circulating,

(3) The printer' from printing and vending copies of the pirated Italian translation.

He would be entitled to this relief during the whole period of British copyright. So much for the translation fraudulently copied from that made by order of the composer. The right to restrain the use of the independent English version would, however, vary according as the facts occurred before or after the expiration of the decennial period. If before, the author might sue the manager of the supposed touring company for an injunction, and the alteration of the work from an opera libretto to a play would not be sufficient to constitute a defence, according to the case of Wood v. Chart. If the ten years had expired before the date of actual or threatened performance he would have no right of action, the translation being *ex hypothesei* an independent one and not a copy.*

[1] Such printing could only have infringement for its object, which distinguishes the case from Farina v. Silverlock, 6 De Gex. Mac and Gordon, p. 214.

L. R. 10 Eq. 193.

* The scene of the public performance of the English libretto is laid beyond the limits of England for the purpose of introducing the question treated of in this note, viz., where the venue of the author's action should be laid. If the plaintiff could discover either by advertisements, handbills, or otherwise before the start of the touring company for their destination that it was the intention of the manager to perform the play in question, an injunction might be obtained in the English Courts. If, on the other hand, the petitioner obtained his knowledge too late to adopt this course, he might apply for an injunction in Dublin.

The following point might arise on the language of articles 5 and 6 of the treaty. The article 5 provides that authors shall have a right of restraining any person unauthorised by them from "making" a translation of their works ("jouissent dans les autres pays du droit exclusif de faire ou d'autoriser la traduction de leurs ouvrages"). The article does not apply to *publication*, but to the *making* of a translation. Suppose then that Mr. Sutherland Edwards or some other skilful translator shortly after the expiration of the ten years sues a thief who may have stolen and reprinted his translation of a French play, could the defendant escape liability by proving from the sequence of dates, cross examination or otherwise, that the petitioner's translation must have been *made* within the ten years, and was therefore not a "traduction licite" within article 6 so as to be entitled to protection, it would seem that as article 6 is framed the wrongdoer would come off scot free.

It was provided by the 15 & 16 Vict., c. 12, s. 6, that nothing in that statute contained should be construed so as to prevent fair representation or adaptations to the English stage of any dramatic piece or musical composition published in any foreign country.

With reference to the question, what is a translation? the case of Wood *v.* Chart is important.

The question arose as to the right of Mr. Wood, the publisher, to restrain the manager of the Brighton Theatre from representing the French comedy of *Frou Frou*. In the piece which purported to be the translation sanctioned by the author, the French plot had been transferred to an English scene, and French names changed into English ones, and many speeches were amplified, altered, or omitted. The question turned upon compliance or non-compliance with the provision in the Act of Parliament and Convention of 1851, to the effect that a translation sanctioned by the author, or a part thereof,

Wood *v.* Chart, 10 Eq. 193.

must be published in the British Dominions within a year after registration and deposit of the original work.

Sir W. M. James, V.C., held in an often quoted judgment that such a conversion from French to English sentiment did not constitute a translation within the meaning of the statute; and that the plaintiff had not complied with the statutory requisitions and could not sue for infringement.

By the 38 Vict., c. 12, Her Majesty was empowered by Order in Council to direct that section 6 of the Act of 1852, as to fair adaptations, should not apply to dramatic pieces first represented in any foreign country. By the Order in Council of the 28th November, 1887, section 6, the last mentioned section was acted upon, and the Berne Convention declares [1] that indirect appropriations such as adaptations, arrangements of music, &c., are especially included among the unlawful reproductions to which the treaty is to apply, when they are only the reproduction of a work in the same form, or in another form, with non-essential alterations, additions, or abridgments so made as not to confer the character of a new original work.

[1] Art. 10.

Article 10 is to be controlled by the law of the forum, but, as has been seen in the case of England, home legislation prepared the way for article 10, so that from henceforth adaptations, such as that in Wood *v.* Chart, will be subject to be restrained. This is in accordance with the view of Vice-Chancellor James in that case when he stated that though the version of *Frou Frou* was not a translation within the meaning of the Act of 1844, it would have been an infringement of the author's copyright.

10 Eq. 206.

OF THE EXTENSION OF INTERNATIONAL COPYRIGHT TO REMOTE POSSESSIONS OF HER MAJESTY.

The International Copyright Act,[1] 1844, treated the colonies and foreign possessions of Her Majesty as for many purposes homogeneous with Great Britain. The recital, expressive of the purposes of the statute, states that the necessity for the Act is found in the inadequacy of previous enactments for assimilating the rights of foreign authors to those of authors of books first published in the "British Dominions;"[2] and the enactments which confer the exclusive right of representation on foreign authors of dramatic pieces and musical compositions extend such exclusive right to any part of "the British Dominions," an expression which, of course, includes all territorial possessions and colonies, wherever situate; and, in like manner, the prohibition against importation of spurious books covered all the territorial possessions of Her Majesty.

Moreover the section[4] which restricts international copyright to that conferred by the statute in question applies to authors of books and dramatic pieces first published out "of Her Majesty's Dominions."

The Statute of 1852 follows the lead of the International Copyright Act, 1844, in incorporating the United Kingdom and the colonies and foreign possessions as one country for the purposes of international copyright. The repealed sections of the last-mentioned Act have been sufficiently referred to in dealing with the subject of translations. Suffice it here to say that the remedies given by way of restraining unauthorised publication of translations, and of preventing unlicensed performance of translated dramatic pieces, all extend to the foreign posses-

[1] 7 Vict., c. 12.
[2] Sec. 5.
[3] Sec. 10.
[4] Sec. 19.
[5] 15 Vict., c. 12.

sions and colonies, as though they and the United Kingdom only constituted one country. Of course, at the same time the question of the forum would not be affected by this doctrine, and the Courts in which to sue an infringer would be those of the colony or possession where the infringement occurs.

The provisions as to registration and deposit of copies all refer, in this statute, to the United Kingdom. No colonial registration or preliminary formalities are contemplated up to this chronological point in the history of international copyright legislation.

In cases, therefore, previous to the International Copyright Act, 1886, and Berne Convention, a foreign author registering in London a piece first performed in a federated country, and also delivering in London a copy of the work in the prescribed manner, would be entitled to sue in respect of any infringement in Melbourne or Calcutta—in the local courts, if the infringer were residing there, in Great Britain if he were to be found within the home limits.

The above observations are chiefly of historical interest, but it is conceivable that cases may occur which would render reference to the old legislation necessary.

The International Copyright Act, 1886,[1] contains provisions specially directed to adjusting *inter se* the rights and liabilities of the United Kingdom and colonies as separate entities. With these provisions we have for the moment nothing to do, as they are distinct from the subject of international copyright, and are treated of in a subsequent section. For the present we have only to consider the triangular position of Great Britain, her colonies, and the extra-territorial nations who may be comprised in any existing or future treaty, such as the Berne Convention, and the relations in which the colonies stand to the mother country when those relations

[1] 49 & 50 Vict., c. 33, s. 8.

are complicated by the presence of a third party to the contract. In construing the Statute of 1886 the definition of "British possession" is important—"any part of Her Majesty's dominions, exclusive of the United Kingdom."

Section 9[1] provides, in effect, that an Order in Council may declare any "British possession" to be excluded from the scope of such or any other order, and of the International Copyright Acts, except so far as is necessary for preventing prejudice to previously-acquired rights; and the expressions in the said Acts relating to Her Majesty's dominions are to be construed accordingly, but save as provided by any such declaration of exclusion, the International Copyright Acts *are to apply to every British possession as if it were part of the United Kingdom.*

<small>'49 & 50 Vict., c. 33, s. 9.</small>

Section 9, taken verbatim, enacts that it shall be lawful by "Order in Council to declare that *such order and the International Copyright Act, and this Act* shall not apply to such British possession." The concluding words of the section enact that "save as provided by such declaration *the said Act and this Act* shall apply to every British possession as if it were part of the United Kingdom."

The latter branch of the section is not the exact converse of the former, which contemplated a declaration excluding the colony from the operation of the Order in Council as well as from the International Copyright Acts; while the concluding words *do not mention the Order in Council*, but only provide that in the absence of a declaration to the contrary *the Acts* shall apply to every British possession as part of the mother country. There would seem to be as good reason for enacting that a convention like, for instance, that of 1887 should *ipso facto* apply to every colony as part of the mother country, as for saying that in certain cases it should not so apply; and it would seem a probable conjecture at first sight that the affirmative enactment was intended to correspond in its scope with the negative one which occurs in the early part of the section; and that the Order in Council is omitted inadvertently from the concluding sentence; but the whole clause is, no doubt, not incapable of a strictly literal construction, the result of which would be that the International Copyright Acts would *ipso facto* apply to the colonies, &c., as part of one country of which the United Kingdom forms another part, while the question whether a colony is brought into the *convention* as a component part of the mother country, or as a separate entity, would depend, not upon the Act, but upon the order itself.

The question, then, now to be considered, is whether the Berne Treaty, and the Order in Council embodying it, apply to the colonies as part of the mother country or as separate countries.

The Treaty of 1887 provides that the federated countries shall have the right to introduce into the Convention their colonies or foreign possessions ("*les pays accédant à la présente convention ont aussi le droit d'y accéder pour leurs colonies ou possessions étrangères*"); the latter words were wisely added having regard to the recent discussions as to the various forms of autonomy, rendering the definition of a "colony" a somewhat vague and uncertain matter. The countries of the Union may declare that all their territorial possessions *en bloc* shall be comprised; or they may single out specific ones which shall be so comprised.

Berne Treaty, Art. 19.

This article was acted upon by Great Britain through a declaration [1] of her representatives appended to the Treaty to the effect that the adhesion ("accession") to the Treaty on her part took in all the colonies and remote possessions of the Queen. They

[1] Procès verbal de signature.

reserved at the same time to the British Government the right to give a notice of determination (under article 20) separately for one or more of the following colonies or possessions:—" India, Canada, Newfoundland, The Cape, Natal, New South Wales, Victoria, Queensland, Tasmania, South Australia, Western Australia, and New Zealand."

The language of article 19 ("*accéder pour ses colonies*") would seem to point to a transaction in which Great **Berne** Britain introduces the colony in question as **Treaty,** part of herself; and this view is strengthened **Art. 19.** when we consider the clauses in which she reserves to herself the power of dislodging hereafter any colony from the scope of the Convention at pleasure. If, then, the colony is to have this homogeneous character with England, and not to rank under the Treaty as a separate state, can it be said that Great Britain is, under article 2, "*the country of origin*," if an opera is composed by a Victorian, and first published at Melbourne? or is the country of origin that which it would certainly seem to be to the popular mind—viz., Australia? The question may have importance from two points of view—viz., with reference to the registration clauses and also to the term of copyright.

As regards the first of these two points, article 2 provides **Berne** that the formalities necessary are those "pre-**Treaty,** scribed by the legislation of the country of **Art. 2.** origin of the work"—in other words, the country where the work is first produced.

Supposing it to be held that Great Britain is the country of origin, what are the "*formalités prescrites par le pays* **49 & 50 Vict.,** *d'origine de l'œuvre*"? We have seen that by **c. 33, s. 4.** the Statute of 1886 the necessity for registration and delivery of copies in the case of a work published in a federated country is abolished, " except so far as provided by the Order" (in the present case, that on which the Berne Treaty is founded). Is then the clause in article 2—"*la jouissance de ces droits est subordonnée à l'accomplissement des conditions et formalités prescrites par la législation du pays d'origine de l'œuvre*"—to be taken as satisfying the words in section 4, "so far as provided by the Order," and as restoring the old registration under the Statute of 1844? If not, it is difficult to give any scope to the words just quoted—unless, indeed, "legislation" refers to future statutory enactment. It is considered by the writers that it will be a prudent precaution, until some authoritative decision be given, to register in the modes prescribed by the Statute of 1844. The provisions of section 8 of the Statute of 1886, which does not deal with international subject-matter, but solely with the relations of Great Britain towards her colonies, would be out of the case. The result is somewhat anomalous; for the purpose of protecting a colonial work in the United Kingdom, or any other part of the British dominions, the registration, &c., must be in the colony, if that colony possesses the necessary machinery. If it is desired to protect a colonial work in one of the other federated countries, it must be registered, and copies be delivered in London. It seems not possible to escape from this result, however whimsical, for the enactments in the Statute of 1886, which exclude the necessity for home registration where a colonial register exists, are clearly only levelled at cases under the Copyright Acts, and do not touch international rights.

If it should be held that the colony is the country of origin of the work under article 2, registration and the other formalities would take place on the spot in the cases where the law of the colony provides for it. In the contrary case, it would

[margin notes: Berne Treaty, Art. 2.; 7 Vict., c. 12, s. 6.; 49 & 50 Vict., c. 33, s. 8.; Berne Treaty, Art. 2.]

not seem that there is anything either in the Act of 1886 or the Convention rendering any such formalities essential.

The question here treated of would be raised by the following state of facts. An author from Mauritius (where, as we assume, there is no necessity for registration) sues under the Berne Treaty in Berlin. He is met by the plea of non-registration. His reply is that there is no necessity for registration in Mauritius. Would the Court uphold the defendant's plea on the ground that Mauritius was part of the mother country for the purposes of the Berne Treaty so as to make British registration necessary, or would it treat Mauritius as the country of origin, in which case no registration would be required?

The question in what character the British possession is to come into the treaty has still more significance when considered in reference to the duration of author's right. Article 2 of the Berne Convention provides that the term is not to exceed that allowed in the country where the work was first produced "*dans le dit pays d'origine.*" In adjusting the rights of Great Britain and her remote possessions we are again obliged to ask what is the meaning of the term "country"? Now the Statute of 1886 [1]authorises the passing in any British possession of any acts or ordinances relating to copyright. Let us assume, then, that the local government of Mauritius, acting under the section last quoted, passes a law adopting the French term of copyright, viz., fifty years from the death of the author. An opera is composed by a native of Mauritius, and first published in that British possession, and the composer seeks to restrain an alleged infringement at Berlin after the expiration of the English term of copyright, but before the termination of the longer Mauritian period. Could not the composer argue with much show of reason that Mauritius was the country of origin of the work, and that the term

[1] Sect. 8, sub-sect. 4.

during which he is entitled to copyright in the other federated countries (in this case Russia) was the longer one? The point is one on which decision may be looked for with interest.

THE LAW OF COPYRIGHT AS BETWEEN GREAT BRITAIN AND THE COLONIES.

We have now to state the present law which regulates the status of the colonies and Great Britain unfettered by the complicating factor of an extra-territorial power.

The Act of 1886 introduces a new departure in that for the first time it treats the colonies as having for some purposes a separate existence from herself.

It is necessary always to bear in mind in construing this Act that the interpretation clause[1] defines "British possession" to mean any part of Her Majesty's dominions exclusive of the United Kingdom, where parts of such dominions are under both a central and local legislature, all parts under one central legislature are for the purposes of this definition deemed to be one British possession. [2] It is enacted that the Copyright Acts are to apply to a literary or artistic work first produced in a *British possession* in like manner as they apply to a work first published in the United Kingdom, but the enactments respecting registration are not to apply where the law of such possession provides for registration, and in the case of a book[3] delivery is no longer necessary at all.

[1] 49 & 50 Vict., c. 33, s. 11.
[2] Sec. 8.
[3] Sub-sect. 1, placitum a.
[3] Sub-sect. 1, placitum b.

It would seem a clear implication from the above that in cases where the law of a British possession does not provide for registration the old enactment in the Copyright Acts will still apply, and registration be still necessary in the home country in order to entitle to copyright any work just published in, say, New Zealand or the Mauritius.

'Where a register of books is kept under the authority of the government of a British possession, an extract from that register, purporting to be certified and authenticated as in the statute provided,² is to be admissible in evidence, and "all courts" (presumably all those of the British possessions, whether home or remote) are to take judicial notice thereof.

<small>¹Sub-sect.2.</small>

<small>² See Appendix.</small>

Where before the passing of the International Copyright Act, 1886,³ an act or ordinance had been passed in any British possession respecting copyright in any literary or artistic works, an order might be made modifying the Copyright Acts or the Act in question, *quâ* works first produced therein.

<small>³Sub-sect.3.</small>

⁴ Nothing in the Copyright Acts or the Act in question is to prevent the passing in a "British possession" of any Act or ordinance respecting copyright within the limits of such possession of works first produced there.

<small>⁴Sub-sect.4.</small>

Under section 8 of the Act of 1886 ⁵ any work first produced in one of Her Majesty's remoter possessions is entitled to protection against infringement in any *British possession* whatever, "whether home or foreign," that being the local range of author's right under the Copyright Acts in a work first produced in the United Kingdom.

<small>⁵Sect. 8, sub-sect. 1 of 49 & 50 Vict., c. 33.</small>

CANADIAN COPYRIGHT.

Considerable attention is now being drawn to the relations between England and Canada in reference to copyright. The Statute of 1886,⁶ in the section which adjusts the rights of England and her

<small>⁶ 49 & 50 Vict., c. 33.</small>

possessions,[1] empowers the colonies to pass an Act or ordinance respecting copyright within the local limits of works first published there. The Canadians are accused of an intention to use this power too arbitrarily; and a proposed new Act (1889)[2] of the local legislature called forth a storm of complaint among the persons in this country who are, or imagine themselves, prejudicially affected; and suggestions were made for resisting the proposed legislation in the interests of British authors and publishers.

In order to explain the gravamen of the charge brought against Canada, it is necessary very shortly to notice some of the legislation which intervened between the dates of the Copyright Amendment Act[3] and the International Copyright Act, 1886.[4] The grievance itself appears to the writers to have enough of substantiality in it to make it a matter of importance to strip off a slight layer of exaggeration which tends to obscure the real point at issue.

It will be remembered that under the Copyright Amendment Act,[5] and a subsequent statute passed three years later,[6] importation into the British dominions of foreign reprints of British works was absolutely prohibited. As regards Canada, however, it is alleged that these enactments proved a dead letter, and that a large trade has been carried on in English copyright works, reprinted in the United States and imported into Canada. In order to mitigate an evil which it appears impossible absolutely to prevent, a statute was passed in the year 1867 which authorised Her Majesty to issue an Order in Council suspending the prohibition against importation. The exercise of this prerogative was subject, however, to a condition precedent, viz., that the

[1] Sec. 8.
[2] The royal assent to this Act has been refused since the following remarks were penned, but they are retained as showing the relations between the Mother Country and the Colony, and because some further attempt may be made to introduce the measure, or an analogous one.
[3] 5 & 6 Vict., c. 45.
[4] 49 & 50 Vict., c. 33.
[5] 5 & 6 Vict., c. 45.
[6] 7 & 8 Vict., c. 12,

Colonial Legislature should have first passed a local statute or ordinance making due provision for protecting in the colony the rights of British authors. Accordingly, with the view of satisfying this condition the Canadian Legislature in the year 1850 passed a local statute under which a duty of 12½ per cent. *ad valorem* was assessed upon foreign reprints of British copyright works imported into Canada, and by an order of the Imperial Council the prohibition as regards Canada was suspended. This state of the law was affirmed by a subsequent Statute of 1868,[1] passed by the Colonial Legislature, and a fresh order of the Imperial Council was issued in the same year; the reason for this supplementary legislation being that doubts had been suggested whether by a certain intermediate enactment[2] in the colony with reference to Custom duties generally, the specific imports relating to copyright works had not been interfered with. Persons imagining themselves aggrieved by the action of the Canadian Parliament go so far as to say that the whole scheme of legislation, both Colonial and Imperial, which has been here sketched out, was part of a deliberate plan to defeat the operation of the Copyright Amendment Act, in so far as it purported to protect British authors. The same objections state that the import of 12½ per cent. was merely offered as an illusory consideration for the suspension of the prohibition against importation, that it never was intended to be, and has never been collected, and, in fact, remains a subsisting debt, either from the Canadian fisc or from the importers distributively. If these be the facts, it is singular that no aggrieved person should have tried the simple experiment of an action in the colony against the importers or (if it be held on the construction of the Act that there is no privity with them) of a petition of right presented to the Canadian Government; the objectors admit, indeed, it is part of their case that no such action has been taken, without, however,

[1] 31 Vict., c. 56.
[2] 31 Vict., c. 7.

assigning any reason for this supineness in action on the part of persons who are not backward in clamorous complaints. The learned writer of an able treatise [1] on this question brands the Statute of 1847 as a sanction to the receiver of stolen goods to reap the benefit of his transactions with the thief, forgetting, in the anxiety to make out a case for British authors, that the title to exclude B from making copies of A's work is only an artificial creature, not founded in any inherent right, but invented, like the testamentary power, for reasons of policy. Remove the prohibition, therefore, and what was only *malum prohibitum*, and not *malum in se*, vanishes. There is no violation of divine or natural law in a Canadian importing, or even selling a book which happens to have been first published in England, any more than in his importing a work first produced in France or America. The statute which imposed a penalty upon such importation once repealed, the stigma of piracy, lavishly imposed by the writer in question, ceases to have any significance.

[1] Anglo-Canadian Copyright by Henry E. Clayton.

The next step in the violent fluctuations to which the intra-territorial copyright law has been incident is a local Statute of 1875, which by a sweeping transition introduced a Canadian copyright in works *reprinted or republished in Canada*, besides maintaining such local copyright as under Acts of the Colonial Legislature would be from time to time enjoyed in respect of works first published there. The Statute of 1875 left the law as to importation as it was—the right to import would therefore remain and the duties would continue to accrue. If the duties have as stated run largely into arrear, let the clamorous British authors who complain that their works have been gratuitously imported, instruct some solicitor on the spot to take the proper action either against the Government or against the individual importers, as they may be advised. The question who is a proper party to be made defendant in such an action may partly depend on Canadian procedure; at all events, the wrong if it exists cannot be one without a remedy—those who do not avail themselves of that remedy have only their own laches to thank.

It will not be forgotten that in a foregoing section the English Copyright Acts are stated to have been made to apply to the colonies and other possessions of Her Majesty as they apply to a work first published in the United Kingdom. Reciprocal rights of suing an infringer are therefore existing in favour of British and Canadian authors. Canada still has the right to import foreign reprints, in which respect no doubt she has an advantage over the United Kingdom, and loud complaints are made by British copyright owners in respect of this alleged inequality. How far she gave adequate consideration for her privileges can only be known when the whole scheme of the legislation passed to adjust the intercolonial rights is thoroughly weighed; possibly the mother country made a bad bargain, but it was probably considered that the $12\frac{1}{2}$ per cent. was a fair measure of remuneration, having regard to the difficulty that would exist in enforcing an absolute law against importation in the case of a frontier like the Canadian one. Indignation was however carried to fever point by the introduction into the Canadian Parliament of a bill[1] which purported to impose, as a condition precedent to the enjoyment of Colonial copyright, registration in the colony before or simultaneously with the publication of a work in any state forming part of the Berne federation.

[1] For the contents of the draft the writers are indebted to the able pamphlet so often cited.

The statute was to extend to British subjects (including, it is presumed, Canadians) and to the natives of the countries other than Great Britain who form part of the Berne union, all of whom were to comply with the registration clause, and were moreover to reprint and republish in Canada within a month of publication elsewhere.

Section 3 enacted (1) that "if the person entitled to copyright under the said Act" (*i.e.*, the Act of 1875) "as hereby amended fails to take advantage of its provision, any person or persons domiciled in Canada may obtain from the Minister of Agriculture a licence or licences to print and publish or to produce the work for which copyright, but for such neglect or failure, might have been obtained; but no such licence shall convey exclusive rights to print and publish or produce any work;" and (2) that "a licence shall be granted to any applicant agreeing to pay the author or his legal representatives a royalty of ten per cent. on the retail price of each copy or reproduction issued of the work which is the subject of the licence, and giving security for such payment to the satisfaction of the Minister."

By section 4 provision is made for the collection of the royalties by the Canadian Inland Revenue; but the Canadian Government was "not to be liable to account for any such royalty not actually collected."

Section 5 provides for prohibiting or allowing the importation of copies of works, as to which licences have been granted according as the licensees do or do not provide adequately for the public demand. And section 6 provides that the Act is not to be taken as prohibiting importation from the United Kingdom of copyright works lawfully published there; nor is it to apply to any work for which copyright has been obtained in the United Kingdom or other countries affected by the Acts before the Act comes into force.

The grounds of complaint from a British point of view against the proposed measure are for the most part stated with great force by the able advocate above mentioned. He appears, however, to be unhappy in that firstly and most prominently put forward, and it may be well to remove this with a view to give prominence to the unanswerable ones which follow.

The first objection is that "the Canadian Courts have decided that the British North America Act of 1867 did not empower the Dominion to legislate against the United Kingdom, so that the Act would be powerless to repeal the provisions of the English Act of 1842. Unless the Dominion Parliament is to be allowed to repeal Acts on the English Statute Book, the Canadian Act is *ipso facto* impossible." One answer which might be given to this point is, that if the Act is "impossible" it can have no operation; the judges would in dealing with any question apply the doctrine of *ultra vires*, and the Dominion Statute would be a dead letter. But the objection is not only unnecessary, it is not borne out by the alleged Canadian decision as stated by the learned author of "Anglo-Canadian copyright" himself. He is obviously referring to the case of Smiles *v.* Bedford, in which an English author who had not *republished or reprinted in Canada* a work first published in the United Kingdom sued for infringement by publication in the colony. The infringers set up unsuccessfully an inferential repeal *pro tanto* of the British Copyright Amendment Act[1] by the Colonial Act of 1875; an argument treated by the learned pamphleteer with scorn, but by no means without strong plausibility when it is considered that the Colonial Act was ratified by and took rank with an Imperial Statute. Prior to judicial decision it might well be supposed that a statute conferring copyright on a certain condition precedent, viz., republication in the colony, was inconsistent with the existence of copyright where such condition was unfulfilled. The Court, however, held that the two Acts were reconcilable, and that in fact an owner of British copyright might elect between the rights conferred by the Copyright Amendment Act, 1845, and those clogged with the conditions imposed by the Canadian Act of 1875. The Judge in the Court below seems to have suggested that the latter statute did not

[1] 5 & 6 Vict., c. 45.

entirely cover the same ground as the Imperial one, inasmuch as a person fulfilling the condition precedent of republication in the colony would be entitled under the Canadian enactment to prevent importation, a remedy which would not be open to a claimant taking his stand on a British copyright under the Copyright Amendment Act, and the *ratio decidendi* was that the two statutes not dealing with precisely the same subject matter did not clash.

According to the statement of the case in the pamphlet, "Anglo-Canadian Copyright," the judges also held "that the British North America Act did not give the Dominion Parliament any right to legislate on copyright questions as against the United Kingdom." This, however, was merely *obiter dictum* and unnecessary, as they also found that there was no collision between the two systems of legislation. The first objection seems really not supported by authority, and is placed on an assailable ground, viz., the very difficult and abstruse proposition how far the colony may legislate in matters relating to its own interest in a sense not parallel with the scheme of imperial enactment. This is written in no spirit of cavil, but from a wish that the force of other more tangible objections should be unimpaired.

The other points made are very short, and in substance as follows: That any legislation at all is unnecessary, because Canada enjoys a position, *quâ* copyright, at least as favourable as the United Kingdom, at all events since the Act of 1886, which purported to settle definitely the rights of the colony, both as regards the mother country and the other federated countries; the proposed statute would be a gratuitous complication and a clog, and one which the other federated countries would resent.

The clauses relating to the royalties and their collection are more unfavourable to authors than those contained in the Acts of 1850 and 1868, and the difficulty of collection would be greater than ever, especially having regard to the clause protecting the Canadian Government from liability in respect of wilful default, which is a new provision, and leaves the copyright proprietor without remedy.

The necessity for registration in Canada is not only a grievous hardship, but is contrary to the whole spirit of the Berne Convention, which pointedly does away with the necessity for any formalities other than those required by the country of origin.

The writers recommend a perusal of the objections, as stated in the pamphlet, where they are given in more detail than would be in keeping with the character of this work. They should be carefully held in reserve against any future attempt to introduce the objectionable law or a modification of it.

APPENDIX I.

AN ACT TO AMEND THE LAW RESPECTING INTERNATIONAL AND COLONIAL COPYRIGHT.—25*th June*, 1886.

Whereas by the International Copyright Acts Her Majesty is authorised by Order in Council to direct that as regards literary and artistic works first published in a foreign country the author shall have copyright therein during the period specified in the order, not exceeding the period during which authors of the like works first published in the United Kingdom have copyright: 49 & 50 Vict., c. 33.

And whereas at an international Conference held at Berne in the month of September, one thousand eight hundred and eighty-five, a draft of a convention was agreed to for giving to authors of literary and artistic works first published in one of the countries parties to the convention copyright in such works throughout the other countries parties to the convention :

And whereas, without the authority of Parliament, such convention cannot be carried into effect in Her Majesty's dominions, and consequently Her Majesty cannot become a party thereto, and it is expedient to enable Her Majesty to accede to the convention :

Be it therefore enacted by the Queen's most Excellent Majesty, by and with the advice and consent of the Lords Spiritual and Temporal, and Commons, in this present Parliament assembled, and by the authority of the same, as follows :

1. (1) This Act may be cited as the International Copyright Act, 1886. Short titles and construction.

(2) The Acts specified in the first part of the first

schedule to this Act are in this Act referred to and may be cited by the short titles in that schedule mentioned, and those Acts, together with the enactment specified in the second part of the said schedule, are in this Act collectively referred to as the International Copyright Acts.

The Acts specified in the second schedule to this Act may be cited by the short titles in that schedule mentioned, and those Acts are in this Act referred to, and may be cited collectively as the Copyright Acts.

(3) This Act and the International Copyright Acts shall be construed together, and may be cited together as the International Copyright Acts, 1844 to 1886.

2. The following provisions shall apply to an Order in Council under the International Copyright Acts :—

Amendment as to extent and effect of order under International Copyright Acts.

(1) The order may extend to all the several foreign countries named or described therein :

(2) The order may exclude or limit the rights conferred by the International Copyright Acts in the case of authors who are not subjects or citizens of the foreign countries named or described in that or any other order, and if the order contains such limitation and the author of a literary or artistic work first produced in one of those foreign countries is not a British subject, nor a subject or citizen of any of the foreign countries so named or described, the publisher of such work, unless the order otherwise provides, shall for the purpose of any legal proceedings in the United Kingdom for protecting any copyright in such work be deemed to be entitled to such copyright as if he were the author, but this enactment shall not prejudice the rights of such author and publisher as between themselves :

(3) The International Copyright Acts and an order made

thereunder shall not confer on any person any greater right or longer term of copyright in any work than that enjoyed in the foreign country in which such work was first produced.

3. (1) An Order in Council under the International Copyright Acts may provide for determining the country in which a literary or artistic work first produced simultaneously in two or more countries, is to be deemed, for the purpose of copyright, to have been first produced, and for the purposes of this section "country" means the United Kingdom and a country to which an order under the said Acts applies. *Simultaneous publication.*

(2) Where a work produced simultaneously in the United Kingdom, and in some foreign country or countries, is by virtue of an Order in Council under the International Copyright Acts deemed for the purpose of copyright to be first produced in one of the said foreign countries, and not in the United Kingdom, the copyright in the United Kingdom shall be such only as exists by virtue of production in the said foreign country, and shall not be such as would have been acquired if the work had been first produced in the United Kingdom.

4. (1) Where an order respecting any foreign country is made under the International Copyright Acts, the provisions of those Acts with respect to the registry and delivery of copies of works shall not apply to works produced in such country except so far as provided by the order. *Modification of certain provisions of International Copyright Acts.*

(2) Before making an Order in Council under the International Copyright Acts in respect of any foreign country, Her Majesty in Council shall be satisfied that that foreign country has made such provisions (if any) as it appears to Her Majesty expedient to require for the protection of authors of works first produced in the United Kingdom.

5. (1) Where a work being a book or dramatic piece is first produced in a foreign country to which an Order in Council under the International Copyright Acts applies, the author or publisher, as the case may be, shall, unless otherwise directed by the order, have the same right of preventing the production in and importation into the United Kingdom of any translation not authorised by him of the said work as he has of preventing the production and importation of the original work.

Restriction on translation.

(2) Provided that if after the expiration of ten years, or any other term prescribed by the order, next after the end of the year in which the work, or in the case of a book published in numbers each number of the book, was first produced, an authorised translation in the English language of such work or number has not been produced, the said right to prevent the production in and importation into the United Kingdom of an unauthorised translation of such work shall cease.

(3) The law relating to copyright, including this Act, shall apply to a lawfully produced translation of a work in like manner as if it were an original work.

(4) Such of the provisions of the International Copyright Act, 1852, relating to translations as are unrepealed by this Act shall apply in like manner as if they were re-enacted in this section.

6. Where an Order in Council is made under the International Copyright Acts with respect to any foreign country, the author and publisher of any literary or artistic work first produced before the date at which such order comes into operation shall be entitled to the same rights and remedies as if the said Acts and this Act and the said order had applied to the said foreign country at the date of the said production : provided that where any person has before the date of the publication

Application of Act to existing works.

of an Order in Council lawfully produced any work in the United Kingdom, nothing in this section shall diminish or prejudice any rights or interests arising from or in connection with such production which are subsisting and valuable at the said date.

7. Where it is necessary to prove the existence or proprietorship of the copyright of any work first produced in a foreign country to which an Order in Council under the International Copyright Acts applies, an extract from a register, or a certificate, or other document stating the existence of the copyright, or the person who is the proprietor of such copyright, or is for the purpose of any legal proceedings in the United Kingdom deemed to be entitled to such copyright, if authenticated by the official seal of a Minister of State of the said foreign country, or by the official seal or the signature of a British diplomatic or consular officer acting in such country, shall be admissible as evidence of the facts named therein, and all courts shall take judicial notice of every such official seal and signature as is in this section mentioned, and shall admit in evidence, without proof, the documents authenticated by it. *Evidence of foreign copyright.*

8. (1) The Copyright Acts shall, subject to the provisions of this Act, apply to a literary or artistic work first produced in a British possession in like manner as they apply to a work first produced in the United Kingdom: *Application of Copyright Acts to colonies.*

Provided that—

   (*a*) The enactments respecting the registry of the copyright in such work shall not apply if the law of such possession provides for the registration of such copyright; and

   (*b*) Where such work is a book the delivery to any persons or body of persons of a copy of any such work shall not be required.

(2) Where a register of copyright in books is kept under the authority of the Government of a British possession, an extract from that register purporting to be certified as a true copy by the officer keeping it, and authenticated by the public seal of the British possession, or by the official seal or the signature of the governor of a British possession, or of a colonial secretary, or of some secretary or minister administering a department of the Government of a British possession, shall be admissible in evidence of the contents of that register, and all courts shall take judicial notice of every such seal and signature, and shall admit in evidence, without further proof, all documents authenticated by it.

(3) Where before the passing of this Act an Act or ordinance has been passed in any British possession respecting copyright in any literary or artistic works, Her Majesty in Council may make an order modifying the Copyright Acts and this Act, so far as they apply to such British possession, and to literary and artistic works first produced therein, in such manner as to Her Majesty in Council seems expedient.

(4) Nothing in the Copyright Acts or this Act shall prevent the passing in a British possession of any Act or ordinance respecting the copyright within the limits of such possession of works first produced in that possession.

9. Where it appears to Her Majesty expedient that an Order in Council under the International Copyright Acts made after the passing of this Act as respects any foreign country, should not apply to any British possession, it shall be lawful for Her Majesty by the same or any other Order in Council to declare that such order and the International Copyright Acts and this Act shall not, and the same shall not, apply to such British possession, except so

Application of International Copyright Acts to colonies.

far as is necessary for preventing any prejudice to any rights acquired previously to the date of such order; and the expressions in the said Acts relating to Her Majesty's dominions shall be construed accordingly; but save as provided by such declaration the said Acts and this Act shall apply to every British possession as if it were part of the United Kingdom.

10. (1) It shall be lawful for Her Majesty from time to time to make Orders in Council for the purposes of the International Copyright Acts and this Act, for revoking or altering any Order in Council previously made in pursuance of the said Acts, or any of them. *Making of Orders in Council.*

(2) Any such Order in Council shall not affect prejudicially any rights acquired or accrued at the date of such order coming into operation, and shall provide for the protection of such rights.

11. In this Act, unless the context otherwise requires—

The expression "literary and artistic work" means every book, print, lithograph, article of sculpture, dramatic piece, musical composition, painting, *Definitions.* drawing, photograph, and other work of literature and art to which the Copyright Acts or the International Copyright Acts, as the case requires, extend.

The expression "author" means the author, inventor, designer, engraver, or maker of any literary or artistic work, and includes any person claiming through the author; and in the case of a posthumous work means the proprietor of the manuscript of such work and any person claiming through him; and in the case of an encyclopædia, review, magazine, periodical work, or work published in a series of books or parts, includes the proprietor, projector, publisher, or conductor.

The expressions "performed" and "performance" and similar words include representation and similar words.

The expression "produced" means, as the case requires, published or made, or, performed or represented, and the expression "production" is to be construed accordingly.

The expression "book published in numbers" includes any review, magazine, periodical work, work published in a series of books or parts, transactions of a society or body, and other books of which different volumes or parts are published at different times.

The expression "treaty" includes any convention or arrangement.

The expression "British possession" includes any part of Her Majesty's dominions exclusive of the United Kingdom; and where parts of such dominions are under both a central and a local legislature, all parts under one central legislature are for the purposes of this definition deemed to be one British possession.

12. The Acts specified in the third schedule to this Act are hereby repealed as from the passing of this Act to the extent in the third column of that schedule mentioned.

Repeal of Acts.

Provided as follows—

(a) Where an Order in Council has been made before the passing of this Act under the said Acts as respects any foreign country, the enactments hereby repealed shall continue in full force as respects that country until the said order is revoked.

(b) The said repeal and revocation shall not prejudice any rights acquired previously to such repeal or revocation, and such rights shall continue and may be enforced in like manner as if the said repeal or revocation had not been enacted or made.

FIRST SCHEDULE.

INTERNATIONAL COPYRIGHT ACTS.

PART I.

SESSION AND CHAPTER.	TITLE.	SHORT TITLE.
7 & 8 Vict., c. 12	An Act to amend the law relating to International Copyright.	The International Copyright Act, 1844.
15 & 16 Vict., c. 12	An Act to enable Her Majesty to carry into effect a Convention with France on the subject of copyright, to extend and explain the International Copyright Acts, and to explain the Acts relating to copyright in engravings.	The International Copyright Act, 1852.
38 & 39 Vict., c. 12	An Act to amend the law relating to International Copyright.	The International Copyright Act, 1875.

PART II.

SESSION AND CHAPTER.	TITLE.	ENACTMENT REFERRED TO.
25 & 26 Vict., c. 68	An Act for amending the law relating to copyright in works of the fine arts, and for repressing the commission of fraud in the production and sale of such works.	Section twelve.

SECOND SCHEDULE.
Copyright Acts.

SESSION AND CHAPTER.	TITLE.	SHORT TITLE.
8 Geo. 2, c. 13	An Act for the encouragement of the arts of designing, engraving, and etching, historical and other prints, by vesting the properties thereof in the inventors and engravers during the time therein mentioned.	The Engraving Copyright Act, 1734.
7 Geo. 3, c. 38	An Act to amend and render more effectual an Act made in the eighth year of the reign of King George the Second, for encouragement of the arts of designing, engraving, and etching, historical and other prints, and for vesting in and securing to Jane Hogarth, widow, the property in certain prints.	The Engraving Copyright Act, 1766.
15 Geo. 3, c. 53	An Act for enabling the two Universities in England, the four Universities in Scotland, and the several Colleges of Eton, Westminster, and Winchester, to hold in perpetuity their copyright in books given or bequeathed to the said universities and colleges for the advancement of useful learning and other purposes of education; and for amending so much of an Act of the eighth year of the reign of Queen Anne, as relates to the delivery of books to the warehouse keeper of the Stationers' Company for the use of the several libraries therein mentioned.	The Copyright Act, 1775.

SESSION AND CHAPTER.	TITLE.	SHORT TITLE.
17 Geo. 3, c. 57	An Act for more effectually securing the property of prints to inventors and engravers by enabling them to sue for and recover penalties in certain cases.	The Prints Copyright Act, 1777.
54 Geo. 3, c. 56	An Act to amend and render more effectual an Act of His present Majesty for encouraging the art of making new models and casts of busts and other things therein mentioned, and for giving further encouragement to such arts.	The Sculpture Copyright Act, 1814.
3 Will. 4, c. 15	An Act to amend the laws relating to Dramatic Literary Property.	The Dramatic Copyright Act, 1833.
5 & 6 Will. 4, c. 65	An Act for preventing the publication of Lectures without consent.	The Lectures Copyright Act, 1835.
6 & 7 Will. 4, c. 69	An Act to extend the protection of copyright in prints and engravings to Ireland.	The Prints and Engravings Copyright Act, 1836.
6 & 7 Will. 4, c. 110	An Act to repeal so much of an Act of the fifty-fourth year of King George the Third, respecting copyrights, as requires the delivery of a copy of every published book to the libraries of Sion College, the four Universities of Scotland, and of the King's Inns in Dublin.	The Copyright Act, 1836.
5 & 6 Vict., c. 45	An Act to amend the law of copyright.	The Copyright Act, 1842.

SESSION AND CHAPTER.	TITLE.	SHORT TITLE.
10 & 11 Vict., c. 95	An Act to amend the law relating to the protection in the Colonies of works entitled to copyright in the United Kingdom.	The Colonial Copyright Act, 1847.
25 & 26 Vict., c. 68	An Act for amending the law relating to copyright in works of the fine arts, and for repressing the commission of fraud in the production and sale of such works.	The Fine Arts Copyright Act, 1862.

THIRD SCHEDULE.

ACTS REPEALED.

SESSION AND CHAPTER.	TITLE.	EXTENT OF REPEAL.
7 & 8 Vict., c. 12	An Act to amend the law relating to international copyright.	Sections fourteen, seventeen, and eighteen.
15 & 16 Vict., c. 12	An Act to enable Her Majesty to carry into effect a Convention with France on the subject of copyright, to extend and explain the International Copyright Acts, and to explain the Acts relating to copyright engravings.	Sections one to five, both inclusive, and sections eight and eleven.
25 & 26 Vict., c. 68	An Act for amending the law relating to copyright in works of the fine arts, and for repressing the commission of fraud in the production and sale of such works.	So much of section twelve as incorporates any enactment repealed by this Act.

APPENDIX II.

At the Court at Windsor, the 28th day of November, 1887,

Present:

The Queen's Most Excellent Majesty,
Lord President,
Lord Stanley of Preston,
Secretary, Sir Henry Holland, Bart.

Whereas the Convention, of which an English translation is set out in the first schedule to this order, has been concluded between Her Majesty the Queen of the United Kingdom of Great Britain and Ireland and the foreign countries named in this Order, with respect to the protection to be given by way of copyright to the authors of literary and artistic works:

And whereas the ratifications of the said Convention were exchanged on the fifth day of September, one thousand eight hundred and eighty-seven, between Her Majesty the Queen and the Governments of the foreign countries following, that is to say:

Belgium, France, Germany, Haïti, Italy, Spain, Switzerland, Tunis.

And whereas Her Majesty in Council is satisfied that the foreign countries named in this Order have made such provisions as it appears to Her Majesty expedient to require for the protection of authors of works first produced in Her Majesty's dominions.

Now, therefore, Her Majesty, by and with the advice of her Privy Council, and by virtue of the authority committed to her by the International Copyright Acts, 1844 to 1886, doth order, and it is hereby ordered as follows:

1. The Convention, as set forth in the first schedule to this Order, shall as from the commencement of this Order, have full effect throughout Her Majesty's dominions, and all persons are enjoined to observe the same.
2. This Order shall extend to the foreign countries following, that is to say:

    Belgium, France, Germany, Haïti, Italy, Spain, Switzerland, Tunis.

    And the above countries are in this Order referred to as the foreign countries of the Copyright Union, and these foreign countries, together with Her Majesty's dominions, are in this Order referred to as "the countries of the Copyright Union."
3. The author of a literary or artistic work, which on or after the commencement of this Order is first produced in one of the foreign countries of the Copyright Union shall, subject as in this Order, and in the International Copyright Acts, 1844 to 1886, mentioned, have as respects that work throughout Her Majesty's dominions the same right of copyright (sic), including any right capable of being conferred by an Order in Council under section 2 or section 5 of the International Copyright Act, 1844, or under any other enactment, as if the work had been first produced in the United Kingdom, and shall have such rights during the same period.

    Provided that the author of a literary or artistic work shall not have any greater right or longer term of copyright therein than that which he enjoys in the country in which the work is first produced.

    The author of any literary or artistic work first

produced before the commencement of this Order shall have the rights and remedies to which he is entitled under section 6 of the International Copyright Act, 1886.

4. The rights conferred by the International Copyright Acts 1844 to 1886 shall, in the case of a literary or artistic work first produced in one of the foreign countries of the Copyright Union by an author who is not a subject or citizen of any of the said foreign countries, be limited as follows: that is to say, the author shall not be entitled to take legal proceedings in Her Majesty's dominions for protecting any copyright in such work, but the publisher of such work shall, for the purpose of any legal proceedings in Her Majesty's dominions for protecting any copyright in such work, be deemed to be entitled to such copyright as if he were the author, but without prejudice to the rights of such author and publisher as between themselves.

5. A literary or artistic work first produced simultaneously in two or more countries of the Copyright Union shall be deemed for the purpose of copyright to have been first produced in that one of those countries in which the term of copyright in the work is shortest.

6. Section 6 of the International Copyright Act, 1852, shall not apply to any dramatic piece to which protection is extended by virtue of this Order.

7. The orders mentioned in the second schedule to this Order are hereby revoked.

   Provided that neither such revocation nor anything else in this Order shall prejudicially affect any right acquired or accrued before the commencement of this Order by virtue of any Order hereby revoked; and any person entitled to such right shall continue entitled thereto, and to the remedies for the same, in like manner as if the Order had not been made.

8. This Order shall be construed as if it formed part of the International Copyright Act, 1886.
9. This Order shall come into operation on the sixth day of December, one thousand eight hundred and eighty-seven, which day is in this Order referred to as the commencement of this Order.

And the Lords Commissioners of Her Majesty's Treasury are to give the necessary orders herein accordingly.

FIRST SCHEDULE.

COPYRIGHT CONVENTION.

Convention for protecting effectively, and in as uniform a manner as possible, the rights of authors over their literary and artistic works. Made on the fifth day of September, one thousand eight hundred and eighty-seven, between Her Majesty the Queen of the United Kingdom of Great Britain and Ireland, Empress of India, His Majesty the German Emperor, King of Prussia, His Majesty the King of the Belgians, Her Majesty the Queen Regent of Spain, in the name of His Catholic Majesty the King of Spain, the President of the French Republic, the President of the Republic of Haïti, His Majesty the King of Italy, the Federal Council of the Swiss Confederation, His Highness the Bey of Tunis.

(The following is an English translation of the Convention, with the omission of the formal beginning and end.)

ARTICLE I.

The Contracting States are constituted into an Union for the protection of the rights of authors over their literary and artistic works.

ARTICLE II.

Authors of any of the countries of the Union, or their lawful representatives, shall enjoy in the other countries for their works, whether published in one of those countries or unpublished, the rights which the respective laws do now or may hereafter grant to natives.

The enjoyment of these rights is subject to the accomplishment of the conditions and formalities prescribed by law in the country of origin of the work, and cannot exceed in the other countries the term of protection granted in the said country of origin.

The country of origin of the work is that in which the work is first published, or if such publication takes place simultaneously in several countries of the Union, that one of them in which the shortest term of protection is granted by law.

For unpublished works the country to which the author belongs is considered the country of origin of the work.

ARTICLE III.

The stipulations of the present Convention apply equally to the publishers of literary and artistic works published in one of the countries of the Union, but of which the authors belong to a country which is not a party to the Union.

ARTICLE IV.

The expression "literary and artistic works" comprehends books, pamphlets, and all other writings; dramatic or dramatico-musical works, musical compositions with or without words; works of design, painting, sculpture, and engraving; lithographs, illustrations, geographical charts; plans, sketches, and plastic works relative to geography, topography, architecture, or science in general; in fact, every production whatsoever in the literary, scientific, or artistic domain which can be published by any mode of impression or reproduction.

ARTICLE V.

Authors of any of the countries of the Union, or their lawful representatives, shall enjoy in the other countries the exclusive right of making or authorising the translation of their works until the expiration of ten years from the publication of the original work in one of the countries of the Union.

For works published in incomplete parts ("livraisons") the period of ten years commences from the date of publication of the last part of the original work.

For works composed of several volumes published at intervals, as well as for bulletins or collections ("cahiers") published by literary or scientific Societies, or by private persons, each volume, bulletin, or collection is, with regard to the period of ten years, considered as a separate work.

In the cases provided for by the present Article, and for the calculation of the period of protection, the 31st December of the year in which the work was published is admitted as the date of publication.

ARTICLE VI.

Authorised translations are protected as original works. They consequently enjoy the protection stipulated in Articles II. and III. as regards their unauthorised reproduction in the countries of the Union.

It is understood that, in the case of a work for which the translating right has fallen into the public domain, the translator cannot oppose the translation of the same work by other writers.

ARTICLE VII.

Articles from newspapers or periodicals published in any of the countries of the Union may be reproduced in original or in translation in the other countries of the Union, unless the authors or publishers have expressly forbidden it. For periodicals it is sufficient if the prohibition is made in a general manner at the beginning of each number of the periodical.

This prohibition cannot in any case apply to articles of political discussion, or to the reproduction of news of the day or *current topics*.

ARTICLE VIII.

As regards the liberty of extracting portions from literary or artistic works for use in publications destined for educational or scientific purposes, or for chrestomathies, the matter is to be decided by the legislation of the different countries of the Union, or by special arrangements existing or to be concluded between them.

ARTICLE IX.

The stipulations of Article II. apply to the public representation of dramatic or dramatico-musical works, whether such works be published or not.

Authors of dramatic or dramatico-musical works, or their lawful representatives, are, during the existence of their exclusive right of translation, equally protected against the unauthorised public representation of translations of their works.

The stipulations of Article II. apply equally to the public performance of unpublished musical works, or of published works in which the author has expressly declared on the title-page or commencement of the work that he forbids the public performance.

ARTICLE X.

Unauthorised indirect appropriations of a literary or artistic work, of various kinds, such as *adaptations, arrangements of music*, &c., are specially included amongst the illicit reproductions to which the present Convention applies, when they are only the reproduction of a particular work, in the same form, or in another form, with non-essential alterations, additions, or abridgments, so made as not to confer the character of a new original work.

It is agreed that, in the application of the present Article, the tribunals of the various countries of the Union will, if there is occasion, conform themselves to the provisions of their respective laws.

ARTICLE XI.

In order that the authors of works protected by the present Convention shall, in the absence of proof to the contrary, be considered as such, and be consequently admitted to institute proceedings against pirates before the Courts of the various countries of the Union, it will be sufficient that their name be indicated on the work in the accustomed manner.

For anonymous or pseudonymous works, the publisher whose name is indicated on the work is entitled to protect the rights belonging to the author. He is, without other proof, reputed the lawful representative of the anonymous or pseudonymous author.

It is, nevertheless, agreed that the Tribunals may, if necessary, require the production of a certificate from the competent authority to the effect that the formalities prescribed by law in the country of origin have been accomplished, as contemplated in Article II.

ARTICLE XII.

Pirated works may be seized on importation into those countries of the Union where the original work enjoys legal protection.

The seizure shall take place conformably to the domestic law of each State.

ARTICLE XIII.

It is understood that the provisions of the present Convention cannot in any way derogate from the right belonging to the Government of each country of the Union to permit, to control, or to prohibit, by measures of domestic legislation or police, the circulation, representation, or exhibition of any works or productions in regard to which the competent authority may find it necessary to exercise that right.

ARTICLE XIV.

Under the reserves and conditions to be determined by common agreement,* the present Convention applies to all works which at the moment of its coming into force have not yet fallen into the public domain in the country of origin.

ARTICLE XV.

It is understood that the Governments of the countries of the Union reserve to themselves respectively the right to enter into separate and particular arrangements between each other, provided always that such arrangements confer upon authors or their lawful representatives more extended rights than those granted by the Union, or embody other stipulations not contrary to the present Convention.

ARTICLE XVI.

An international office is established, under the name of "Office of the International Union for the Protection of Literary and Artistic Works."

This Office, of which the expenses will be borne by the Administrations of all the countries of the Union, is placed under the high authority of the Superior Administration of the Swiss Confederation, and works under its direction. The functions of this Office are determined by common accord between the countries of the Union.

* See paragraph 4 of Final Protocol, p. 138.

ARTICLE XVII.

The present Convention may be submitted to revisions in order to introduce therein amendments calculated to perfect the system of the Union.

Questions of this kind, as well as those which are of interest to the Union in other respects, will be considered in Conferences to be held successively in the countries of the Union by Delegates of the said countries.

It is understood that no alteration in the present Convention shall be binding on the Union except by the unanimous consent of the countries composing it.

ARTICLE XVIII.

Countries which have not become parties to the present Convention, and which grant by their domestic law the protection of rights secured by this Convention, shall be admitted to accede thereto on request to that effect.

Such accession shall be notified in writing to the Government of the Swiss Confederation, who will communicate it to all the other countries of the Union.

Such accession shall imply full adhesion to all the clauses and admission to all the advantages provided by the present Convention.

ARTICLE XIX.

Countries acceding to the present Convention shall also have the right to accede thereto at any time for their Colonies or foreign possessions.

They may do this either by a general declaration comprehending all their Colonies or possessions within the accession, or by specially naming those comprised therein, or by simply indicating those which are excluded.

ARTICLE XX.

The present Convention shall be put in force three months after the exchange of the ratifications, and shall remain in effect for an indefinite period until the termination of a year from the day on which it may have been denounced.

Such denunciation shall be made to the Government authorised to receive accessions, and shall only be effective as regards the country making it, the Convention remaining in full force and effect for the other countries of the Union.

ARTICLE XXI.

The present Convention shall be ratified, and the ratifications exchanged at Berne, within the space of one year at the latest.

In witness whereof, the respective Plenipotentiaries have signed the same, and have affixed thereto the seal of their arms.

Done at Berne, the 9th day of September, 1886.

(Signed by the various Plenipotentiaries.)

ADDITIONAL ARTICLE.

The Plenipotentiaries assembled to sign the Convention concerning the creation of an International Union for the protection of literary and artistic works have agreed upon the following Additional Article, which shall be ratified together with the Convention to which it relates:—

The Convention concluded this day in no wise affects the maintenance of existing Conventions between the Contracting States, provided always that such Conventions confer on authors, or their lawful representatives, rights more extended than those secured by the Union, or contain other stipulations which are not contrary to the said Convention.

In witness whereof, the respective Plenipotentiaries have signed the present Additional Article.

Done at Berne, the 9th day of September, 1886.

(Signed as before.)

FINAL PROTOCOL.

In proceeding to the signature of the Convention concluded this day, the undersigned Plenipotentiaries have declared and stipulated as follows:

1. As regards Article IV., it is agreed that those countries of the Union where the character of artistic works is not refused to photographs, engage to admit them to the benefits of the Convention concluded to-day, from the date of its coming into effect. They are, however, not bound to protect the authors of such works further than is permitted by their own legislation, except in the case of international engagements already existing, or which may hereafter be entered into by them.

It is understood that an authorised photograph of a protected work of art shall enjoy legal protection in all the countries of the Union, as contemplated by the said Convention, for the same period as the principal right of reproduction of the work itself subsists, and within the limits of private arrangements between those who have legal rights.

2. As regards Article IX., it is agreed that those countries of the Union whose legislation implicitly includes choregraphic works amongst dramatico-musical works, expressly admit the former works to the benefits of the Convention concluded this day.

It is, however, understood that questions which may arise on the application of this clause shall rest within the competence of the respective Tribunals to decide.

3. It is understood that the manufacture and sale of instruments for the mechanical reproduction of musical airs which are copyright, shall not be considered as constituting an infringement of musical copyright.

4. The common agreement alluded to in Article XIV. of the Convention is established as follows:—

The application of the Convention to works which have not fallen into the public domain at the time when it comes into force, shall operate according to the stipulations on this head which may be contained in special Conventions either existing or to be concluded.

In the absence of such stipulations between any countries of the Union, the respective countries shall regulate, each for itself, by its domestic legislation, the manner in which the principle contained in Article XIV. is to be applied.

5. The organisation of the International Office established in virtue of Article XVI. of the Convention shall be fixed by a Regulation which shall be drawn up by the Government of the Swiss Confederation.

The official language of the International Office will be French.

The International Office will collect all kinds of information relative to the protection of the rights of authors over their literary and artistic works. It will arrange and publish such information. It will study questions of general utility likely to be of interest to the Union, and, by the aid of documents placed at its disposal by the different Administrations, will edit a periodical publication in the French language, treating questions which concern the Union. The Governments of the countries of the Union reserve to themselves the faculty of authorising, by common accord, the publication by the Office of an edition in one or more other languages if experience should show this to be requisite.

The International Office will always hold itself at the disposal of members of the Union, with the view to furnish them with any special information they may require relative to the protection of literary and artistic works.

The administration of the country where a Conference is about to be held will prepare the programme of the Conference with the assistance of the International Office.

The Director of the International Office will attend the

sittings of the Conferences, and will take part in the discussions without a deliberative voice. He will make an annual Report on his administration, which shall be communicated to all the members of the Union.

The expenses of the Office of the International Union shall be shared by the Contracting States. Unless a fresh arrangement be made, they cannot exceed a sum of 60,000 fr. a year. This sum may be increased by the decision of one of the Conferences provided for in Article XVII.

The share of the total expense to be paid by each country shall be determined by the division of the Contracting and acceding States into six classes, each of which shall contribute in the proportion of a certain number of units, viz. :—

First Class	25 units.
Second ,,	20 ,,
Third ,,	15 ,,
Fourth ,,	10 ,,
Fifth ,,	5 ,,
Sixth ,,	3 ,,

These coefficients will be multiplied by the number of States of each class, and the total product thus obtained will give the number of units by which the total expense is to be divided. The quotient will give the amount of the unity of expense.

Each State will declare, at the time of its accession, in which of the said classes it desires to be placed.

The Swiss Administration will prepare the Budget of the Office, superintend its expenditure, make the necessary advances, and draw up the annual account, which shall be communicated to all the other Administrations.

6. The next Conference shall be held at Paris between four and six years from the date of the coming into force of the Convention.

The French Government will fix the date within these limits after having consulted the International Office.

7. It is agreed that, as regards the exchange of ratifications contemplated in Article XXI., each Contracting Party shall give a single instrument, which shall be deposited, with those of the other States, in the Government archives of the Swiss Confederation. Each party shall receive in exchange a copy of the *procès verbal* of the exchange of ratifications, signed by the Plenipotentiaries present.

The present Final Protocol, which shall be ratified with the Convention concluded this day, shall be considered as forming an integral part of the said Convention, and shall have the same force, effect, and duration.

In witness whereof the respective Plenipotentiaries have signed the same.

Done at Berne, the 9th day of September, 1886.

(Signed as before.)

PROCÈS VERBAL OF SIGNATURE.

The undersigned Plenipotentiaries, assembled this day to proceed with the signature of the Convention with reference to the creation of an International Union for the protection of literary and artistic works, have exchanged the following declarations :—

1. With reference to the accession of the Colonies or foreign possessions provided for by Article XIX. of the Convention :

The Plenipotentiaries of His Catholic Majesty the King of Spain reserve to the Government the power of making known His Majesty's decision at the time of the exchange or ratifications.

The Plenipotentiary of the French Republic states that the accession of his country carries with it that of all the French Colonies.

The Plenipotentiaries of Her Britannic Majesty state

that the accession of Great Britain to the Convention for the protection of literary and artistic works comprises the United Kingdom of Great Britain and Ireland, and all the Colonies and foreign possessions of Her Britannic Majesty.

At the same time they reserve to the Government of Her Britannic Majesty the power of announcing at any time the separate denunciation of the Convention by one or several of the foreign Colonies or possessions, in the manner provided for by Article XX. of the Convention, namely :—

India, the Dominion of Canada, Newfoundland, the Cape, Natal, New South Wales, Victoria, Queensland, Tasmania, South Australia, Western Australia, and New Zealand.

2. With respect to the classification of the countries of the Union having regard to their contributory part to the expenses of the International Bureau (No. 5 of the Final Protocol) :

The Plenipotentiaries declare that their respective countries should (sic) be ranked in the following classes, namely :—

>Germany in the first class.
>Belgium in the third class.
>Spain in the second class.
>France in the first class.
>Great Britain in the first class.
>Haïti in the fifth class.
>Italy in the first class.
>Switzerland in the third class.
>Tunis in the sixth class.

The Plenipotentiary of the Republic of Liberia states that the powers which he has received from his Government authorise him to sign the Convention, but that he has not received instructions as to the class in which his country proposes to place itself with respect to the contribution to the expenses of the International Bureau. He therefore

APPENDIX.

reserves that question to be determined by his Government, who will make known their intention on the exchange of ratifications.

In witness whereof, the respective Plenipotentiaries have signed the present *procès verbal.*

Done at Berne, the 9th day of September, 1886.

(Signed as before.)

PROCÈS VERBAL RECORDING DEPOSIT OF RATIFICATIONS.

In accordance with the stipulations of Article XXI., paragraph 1, of the Convention for the creation of an International Union for the protection of literary and artistic works, concluded at Berne on the 9th September, 1886, and in consequence of the invitation addressed to that effect by the Swiss Federal Council to the Governments of the High Contracting Parties, the undersigned assembled this day in the Federal Palace at Berne for the purpose of examining and depositing the ratifications of :—

Her Majesty the Queen of Great Britain and Ireland, Empress of India,

His Majesty the Emperor of Germany, King of Prussia,

His Majesty the King of the Belgians,

Her Majesty the Queen Regent of Spain, in the name of His Catholic Majesty the King of Spain,

The President of the French Republic,

The President of the Republic of Haïti,

His Majesty the King of Italy,

The Council of the Swiss Confederation,

His Highness the Bey of Tunis,

to the said International Convention, followed by an Additional Article and Final Protocol.

The instruments of these acts of ratification having been produced and found in good and due form, they have been delivered into the hands of the President of the Swiss Confederation, to be deposited in the archives of the

Government of that country, in accordance with clause No. 7 of the Final Protocol of the International Convention.

In witness whereof the undersigned have drawn up the present *procès verbal*, to which they have affixed their signatures and the seals of their arms.

Done at Berne, the 5th September, 1887, in nine copies, one of which shall be deposited in the archives of the Swiss Confederation with the instruments of ratification.

(Signed as before.)

PROTOCOL.

On proceeding to the signature of the *procès verbal* recording the deposit of the acts of ratification given by the High Parties Signatory to the Convention of the 9th September, 1886, for the creation of an International Union for the protection of literary and artistic works, the Minister of Spain renewed, in the name of his Government, the declaration recorded in the *procès verbal* of the Conference of the 9th September, 1886, according to which the accession of Spain to the Convention includes that of all the territories dependent upon the Spanish Crown.

The undersigned have taken note of this declaration.

In witness whereof they have signed the present Protocol, done at Berne, in nine copies, the 5th September, 1887.

(Signed as before.)

SECOND SCHEDULE.

ORDERS IN COUNCIL REVOKED.

Orders in Council of the dates named below for securing the privileges of copyright in Her Majesty's dominions to authors of works of literature and the fine arts, and dramatic pieces, and musical compositions first produced in the following foreign countries, namely:—

FOREIGN COUNTRY.	DATE OF ORDER.
Prussia	27th August, 1846.
Saxony	26th September, 1846.
Brunswick	24th April, 1847.
The States of the Thuringian Union	10th August, 1847.
Hanover	30th October, 1847.
Oldenburg	11th February, 1848.
France	10th January, 1852.
Anhalt, Dessau and Analt Bernbourg (sic)	11th March, 1853.
Hamburgh	25th November, 1853, and 8th July, 1855.
Belgium	8th February, 1855.
Prussia, Saxony, Saxe-Weimar	19th October, 1855.
Spain	24th September, 1857, and 20th November, 1880.
The States of Sardinia	4th February, 1861.
Hesse Darmstadt	5th February, 1862.
Italy	9th September, 1865.
German Empire	24th September, 1886.

The Order in Council of 5th August, 1875, revoking the application of section 6 of 15 and 16 Victoria, chapter 12, to dramatic pieces, referred to in the Order in Council of 10th January, 1852, with respect to works first published in France

APPENDIX III.

FORMS OF AGREEMENT FOR SALES OF COPYRIGHT, LICENCES, ETC.

RECEIPT ON SALE OF A COPYRIGHT OF A SONG OR PIECE OF MUSIC FOR A SUM PAID DOWN.

London_____18

Received of A B, of No._____Street, London, the sum of_____ for the absolute purchase of all my Copyright, right of representation, and other rights, present and future, throughout the United Kingdom of Great Britain and Ireland, and the Colonies and dependencies thereof, and also all foreign countries, in and of the_____ entitled_____

and I declare that the said A B shall be entitled to arrange and use the melody in any separate musical composition which_____may publish without any further payment or consideration whatever.

£   :   :

MEMORANDUM OF SALE OF COPYRIGHT IN A SONG OR PIECE OF MUSIC.

Memorandum.—That I_____ of_____ in consideration of the price or sum of_____

have this day sold and assigned, and do hereby sell and assign absolutely to_____and_____ of_____ Street, London, Music Publishers, trading under the firm of_____all my right, title, copyright, right of performance, and interest of whatsoever kind, for Great Britain, Ireland, her Colonies and dependencies, and for every other country in respect of which there is at present, or may be in future, a convention

with Great Britain as to copyright, and right of representation, of and in_____
_____
_____
_____

being solely my property.

    And I hereby agree that the said _____and_____ shall be entitled to use and publish the said work, or any portion thereof, in any other separate form, free from any consideration whatsoever in respect of such use and publication.

    Witness my hand and seal this_____day of_____ in the Year of our Lord One Thousand Eight Hundred and_____

Signed, Sealed, and Delivered }
    in the presence of   }

_____

_____

(L. S.)

London_____ 18

Received of Messrs. _____and_____ the sum of _____Pounds,_____shillings, _____pence, above mentioned.

£   :   :

RECEIPT ON SALE OF A COPYRIGHT OF A SONG OR PIECE OF MUSIC IN CONSIDERATION OF A SUM PAID DOWN AND A ROYALTY.

London _____ 18

Received of A B, of No._____Street, London, the sum of_____ for the absolute purchase of all my Copyright, right of representation, and other rights, present and future, throughout the United Kingdom of Great Britain and Ireland, and the Colonies and dependencies thereof, and also all foreign countries, in and of the_____ entitled_____

_____

    Subject, however, to, and charged in the hands of every assignee with a Royalty of_____d. per copy, on each copy of the Song sold, after the first_____and with the usual allowance of 7 copies as 6.

K 2

It is, however, understood and agreed that the Royalty aforesaid shall not apply to or be charged on any pianoforte or other arrangement of the said work, and that accordingly the said A B shall be entitled to arrange and use the melody of the said work in any separate musical composition or arrangement as_____may think fit, and to print, publish, and sell the same, and shall not be liable to pay any Royalty or other consideration for so doing.

£   :   :

MEMORANDUM OF SALE OF COPYRIGHT IN A SONG OR PIECE OF MUSIC. CONSIDERATION, A SUM PAID DOWN AND A ROYALTY. SPECIAL AGREEMENT AS TO CANADIAN COPIES.

In consideration of the price or sum of_____ paid to me this day; and in addition to a Royalty of_____pence per copy hereby agreed to be paid to me on all copies printed and sold, with the exception of the first_____hundred copies in each key, in which the under-mentioned work shall be published; which said copies shall be free from any Royalty, for the purpose of circulation.

And it is also further agreed that every seventh copy of the said work afterwards published shall be freed from the above-mentioned Royalty, for the purpose of trade supply, and on any copies printed, by my consent, for sale in the United States, there shall be no Royalty payable to me

Should any agreement be made for this work with the_____, _____, I agree to accept on their Edition for circulation in Canada only, a Royalty of One Penny per copy, allowing them free from Royalty the first fifty copies.

On these terms, I,_____ of_____ have this day sold and assigned, and do hereby sell and assign absolutely to Mr._____and Mr._____of_____Street, London, Music Publishers, trading under the firm of_____all my right, title, copyright, right of performance, and interest of whatsoever kind, for Great Britain, Ireland, her Colonies and dependencies, and for every other country in which there is at present, or may be in future, a mutual International convention in respect of copyright, and right of representation thereof, of and in____ _ ___ . _ _ -

Subject, however, and charged with the payment of the said Royalty into whosesoever hands the said premises hereby assigned shall come.

And I hereby agree that the said _____ and _____ shall be entitled to use and publish the said work, or any portion thereof, in any other separate form, free from any consideration whatsoever in respect of such use and publication.

It is also agreed that the said _____ and _____ shall keep a regular account of the publication and sale of the copies of the said work, and shall render me a statement on or after the _____ day of _____ and the _____ day of _____ in each year.

Witness my hand and seal this _____ day of _____ in the Year of our Lord One Thousand Eight Hundred and _____

Signed, Sealed, and Delivered }
   in the presence of   }

_____

_____

(L. S.)

                    London _____ 18

Received of Messrs. _____ and _____ the sum of _____ Pounds, _____ shillings, _____ pence, above mentioned.

£   :   :

DEED OF ASSIGNMENT IN CONSIDERATION OF A SUM PAID DOWN AND A ROYALTY. THE PUBLISHER UNDERTAKING TO KEEP ACCOUNTS, WHICH CAN BE INSPECTED BY THE AUTHOR.

This Indenture made the _____ day of _____ 18 **Between** _____ of _____ in the County of _____ (hereinafter called "the author") of the one part, and _____ of _____ in the County of _____ Music Publisher (hereinafter called "the purchaser") of the other part. **Witnesseth**

(1) In consideration of £ _____ this day paid by the purchaser to the author (the receipt whereof the author hereby acknowledges) and of the Royalty hereinafter mentioned, the author hereby assigns to the purchaser all his copyright and interest of every kind, present and future (including the right of representation), of and in the _____ entitled _____

(2) In addition to the said sum of £ _____ the purchaser, and every

assignee of the copyright for the time being, shall pay to the author a Royalty of _____ pence per copy on all copies of the said _____ printed and sold by him after the first _____ copies.

(3) For all purposes hereof 7 copies shall be counted as 6.

(4) The purchaser shall keep true accounts of all copies sold by him, which shall be open to the inspection of the author, or his agent authorised in writing, at all reasonable times.

(5) The author may at any time, at his own cost, require the purchaser to make a statutory declaration of the number of copies sold; but in such case such statutory declaration shall, for all purposes of the Royalty, be absolutely binding on the author.*

In witness, &c.

_____,

_____ (L. S.)

AGREEMENT BETWEEN AN AUTHOR AND A PERSON WISHING TO TRANSLATE HIS WORK.

An Agreement made this _____ day of _____ 18__ Between A B of _____ _____ in the County of _____ (hereinafter called "the author") of the one part, and C D of _____ in the County of _____ _____ (hereinafter called "the translator") of the other part.

Whereas the author has written and published in the French language a play, entitled _____

And whereas the translator has applied to the author to allow him to translate into the English language and adapt to the English stage the said play, which the author hath agreed to do upon the following terms, namely (*here insert provisions, acts, payment, &c.*).

LICENCE BY PROPRIETOR OF COPYRIGHT IN A PLAY.

I _____ of _____ in the County of _____ being the owner of the Copyright in the Drama or Play called _____ do hereby grant to _____ of _____ in the County of _____ the sole and exclusive right of representing the said play within a distance of 12 miles from Temple Bar, London, for the space of _____ years from the date herein, in consideration of the sum of £ _____ by the said _____ paid to me, the receipt whereof I do hereby acknowledge.

Dated this _____ day of _____ 18__

To Mr. _____

---

* This clause is uncommon, but has been found by one of the writers to be very convenient in practice.

SPECIMEN FORMS TO BE INSERTED IN AGREEMENTS.

Commencement.
An Agreement made this _____ day of _____ 18
Between A B of _____ in the County of _____
(hereinafter called "the author") of the one part and
C D of _____ in the County of _____
(hereinafter called $\begin{Bmatrix}\text{"the publisher"}\\\text{"the manager"}\end{Bmatrix}$ of the other part,
whereby it is mutually agreed as follows—

Where work not yet written.
The author agrees to write and edit a work to be called _____

Or not completed.
The author has partly written a work to be called _____
which he hereby agrees to completely finish and edit.

When work completely written.
The author has written a work on the _____
which he hereby agrees to edit.

And ready for press.
Whereas the author has written and composed a work on the _____
entitled _____
and the same is now ready to be printed and published.

Agreement to write a play or opera.
Whereas the $\begin{Bmatrix}\text{publisher}\\\text{manager}\end{Bmatrix}$ has applied to the author to write for him for the purpose of being produced at the _____ Theatre, a $\begin{Bmatrix}\text{drama}\\\text{opera}\end{Bmatrix}$ which the author has agreed to do upon the following terms :—

Author to deliver MS. by a specified day and to correct proof sheets.
The author shall prepare the said work for press, and deliver the same to the publisher ready for printing on or before the _____ day of _____ next, and shall correct the proof sheets.

Author sells all Copyright to publisher.
The author sells and assigns to the publisher all Copyright, British, Colonial, and International, in the said work (or in the first edition of the said work).

All costs of corrections, &c., in proof sheets, beyond a specified amount to be paid by the author.
All alterations and corrections in the proof sheets which shall on the average exceed _____ per sheet shall be borne and paid by the author.

Publisher to print and publish.
The publisher will at his own expense print and publish the said work.

Publisher to pay a single sum as purchase money.	The publisher will, on the day of publication of the said work, pay to the author the sum of £_____ as the purchase money of the said copyright.
Or a Royalty.	The publisher will pay to the author a Royalty of _____ a copy for copies of the work sold (copies sold being counted as hereinafter mentioned).
Costs of printing, publishing, &c., to be deducted from gross sales and the remainder to be considered as profit.	All costs of printing and publishing the said work, including all costs of printing, paper, advertisements, embellishments (if any), and other incidental expenses, and including the allowance of ____ per cent. on the gross amount of the sale for commission, and of ____ per cent. for bad debts, shall be deducted from the gross amount of the sales of the said work, and any amount remaining after such deduction shall be considered to be profit.
Profits to be divided.	The profits shall be divided between the author and publisher in the following proportions, namely, to the author .... _____ _____ ____ and to the publisher
Publisher to keep and render true accounts.	The publisher shall keep true accounts of the sales of the said work and of all deductions to be made therefrom. Such accounts shall be open to the inspection of the author or one agent, to be appointed by him by writing, at all reasonable times. In addition, the publisher shall render half-yearly accounts to the author on the_____ day of_____ and the_____ day of_____ in every year, showing the amount of sales and deductions, and with such accounts shall pay to the author the balance thereby shown to be due to him.
Sales to be subject to usual trade discount.	The books sold shall be accounted for, less the usual trade discount and 13 copies being reckoned as 12.
Another form.	The publisher shall account to the author for all copies sold at wholesale prices, the publisher bearing all risk of bad debts, and being entitled to a commission of _____ per cent. for so doing.
Author to have the right to require the publisher to verify his account by a statutory declaration.	The publisher shall, if required by the author so to do by notice in writing, make out an account of all receipts and payments by him on account of the said work, and shall make a statutory declaration that all receipts and payments by him on account of the said work are truly stated in the said account, and the account when so verified shall be complete and binding between the parties.

NOTE.—A question has sometimes been raised on the construction of assignments of copyright, whether a clause providing for the payment of a royalty to the author or composer is inseparably annexed to the copyright, so that the liability to pay it passes to a sub-purchaser; or constitutes a mere collateral obligation personally binding on the original purchaser only. In order that the copyright should be charged with the burden in the hands of the possessor for the time being, two things are necessary—(1) that there should be an intention to that effect manifested in the original assignment; (2) that the subsequent assignee sought to be charged should have had notice of this fact when he bought. The point is the more important as an erroneous impression seems to exist in the minds of music publishers and composers that copyright is effectually saddled with a royalty under an agreement containing (a) an assignment by A to B of the copyright, (b) an agreement by B to pay A so much per copy sold. There is no authority that an instrument framed on this principle would import any more than a personal undertaking by B, who, if he parted with the copyright to C, would not at the same time divest himself of his liability to pay the royalty. The principle is stated in the report of Werderman *v.* Société Générale d'Électricité, 19 Ch. div. 246; where the question arose on the closely analogous case of a patent. The precedents in this work are so framed as to charge the copyright in the hands of sub-purchasers.

APPENDIX IV.

The old copyright laws of the United States provided that no person not a citizen or resident should enjoy a copyright in America. This was not left merely to inference or judicial decision, the right to reap in the alien's field was preserved to natives by express statutory enactment. Readers of the *Times* of the last two years are familiar with the state of literary commerce which was the outcome of this shortsighted policy. American publishers have had it in their power to print off at a reduced cost the works of Lord Tennyson or Miss Braddon; and so to flood the market with cheap literature and render impossible competition by American authors. It has been discovered at last that what had appeared to superficial thinkers to be a source of gain to the States, in reality operated disastrously not only to the cause of literature in the abstract, but also to the better class of American publishers. The houses in the Eastern States had, it is true, come to an informal agreement restraining competition *inter se* as regarded any work printed abroad of which one of them had obtained advance sheets; but the publishers of the rapidly growing States of Chicago and San Francisco could not be controlled from a distance; and the publishing business degenerated at length into a mere scramble; the respectable publishers endeavouring to bring out a reprint of an English popular work with a rapidity prejudicial to the style of the publication in order to outstrip enterprising spirits, who, relying on the judgment of the larger houses for the choice of subject matter, employed authors to write against time some work similar in name and character to that of which the advance sheets only had reached America, and were being reprinted by the better class of editor whom capital and influence had enabled to get a start. The larger houses were in the end beaten in the race; prices had to be reduced lower and lower, some editors abandoned the production of American fiction owing to the ruinous competition of cheap reprints of English works; even such reprints ceased to be remunerative. Out of evil cometh good. The American copyright law as regards relations with foreigners has at length been revised to the extent necessary for the advance of American interests, and this new departure works collateral benefit to the authors of Great Britain. The result has been brought about by an Act which came into operation on the 1st July, 1891. In lieu of the obnoxious section above referred to legalising plunder of the foreigner, a clause has been introduced enabling him to acquire copyright on certain conditions as to printing which are stated below.

<small>Revised Statutes, sec. 4971.</small>

The benefits of the new Act are extended to a citizen of a foreign state when such foreign state permits to Americans the "benefit of copyright on substantially the same basis as its own citizens," or when such foreign state is a party to an International agreement which provides for reciprocity in the granting of copyright by the terms of which agreement the United States are at liberty to become a party thereto. The President is to determine the existence of either of these conditions by proclamation. The English law officers have given a certificate to the effect that England falls within the first alternative condition, involving, it is apprehended, the proposition that according to that law it is no longer necessary that a foreigner should be actually resident in the British dominions in order to entitle him to copyright in a work first published by him here; for the American law does not require that the foreigner should be resident in America. The

<small>Sec. 13.</small>

President has accordingly proclaimed that this country comes within the purview of the Act of 1891. An impression exists in the minds of some continental authors not natives of States forming part of the Berne convention, that by originally publishing in Great Britain and America simultaneously they may obtain American copyright; and applications to undertake such first publication as agents for the applicants are being made to London publishing firms. Such a step would be useless for the object proposed; and arises from a fallacy finding a resemblance between the American statute of 1891 and the Berne Convention where none such exists. Article 3 of that document brings in works published in one of the countries of the Union though the authors may be strangers to it, but this has no parallel in the law of the United States, under which, in order to be admitted to copyright, the author must be citizen of a state which gives reciprocal rights to America; publication of the work in such a state, even accompanied by simultaneous publication in the United States, confers no right under American law. It would seem that a sale and assignment by the non-privileged author to the London publisher would enable the latter to obtain American copyright.

The principal section of this statute is a repetition of a cognate clause of the Act of the 8th July, 1870; the only alteration being that the words confining the benefit of the section to the American citizens or residents in America are struck out. As altered, it enacts in effect that authors or proprietors "of any book, map, chart, dramatic or musical composition, engraving, cut, print, or photograph, or negative thereof" ... shall, upon complying with the provisions of the statute, have the sole liberty of printing, reprinting, publishing, completing, copying, executing, finishing and vending the same; and in the case of dramatic composition, of publicly performing or representing it:" and authors or their assigns shall have exclusive right to dramatise and translate any of their copyrighted works." American Statute of 1891, Revised Statutes, sec. 4952.

The Act, then, applies to any book, dramatic or musical composition, and comprises the exclusive right:—(*a*) Of reproducing and translating any works. (*b*) Of performing dramatic pieces.

The performing right of music has never been treated as of much importance in America, and it is advisedly omitted.

The term of copyright is twenty-eight years from the time of recording the title. The mode of complying with the requirements in this respect will be treated of below.

The Act empowers a prolongation for the further term of fourteen years, subject to the title being recorded a second time, and to all other regulations in regard to original copyright being complied with within six months from the expiration of the first term. Sec. 4954.

The mode of recording the title is given in a section which, both before and since the passing of the Act, has been the subject of much discussion. The section, to a great extent, speaks for itself, but comment in some detail on portions of it which raise question will be found useful to the many English authors and publishers who will now copyright their works in the United States. The first point which occurs to the student is that the delivery of copies of the title and work are not merely conditions precedent to a right to sue, as with us, but that the very existence of copyright depends upon their fulfilment. It is clear that, according to the American law, no right attaches till these acts have been performed. Sec. 4956.
Drone on Copyright. p. 265.

A printed copy of the title of the work is to be deposited. The American practice allows the mere deposit of a type-written description of the title. Some large firms enter the whole title-page, but the name of the work is sufficient. "Two copies of such copyright book, map, chart, dramatic or musical composition, engraving, chromo, cut, print, or photograph" . . . are to be delivered.

Time of Delivery.

The delivery of the copy of title is to be made on or before the day of publication in this or any foreign country.

¹ Boucicault v. Hart, 13, Blatch. 47, Drone, 284.

The delivery of copies of the work is to take place "not later than the day of publication thereof in this or any foreign country." The American Courts have laid down that in the absence of any direct enactment, the publication must take place within a reasonable time after recording the title. In one case in America the interval between October 24th and the following February was held to be an unreasonable time, and the copyright was lost.[1]

An important point for the consideration of English authors wishing to acquire copyright in America arises here. It has been held in America that

² Wall v. Gordon Drone, 296.

an author forfeits his claim to copyright there by a first publication of his work abroad, but not by a contemporaneous one.[2] The only mode in which an Englishman can secure copyright in America and Great Britain also is by simultaneous publication in the two countries, and delivery of copies of title and of the work not later than the date of that publication. In either

4956.

country prior publication in the other will defeat the privilege. The section contains a proviso that in the case of a "*book, photograph, chromo, or lithograph*," the two copies of the same required to be delivered "shall be printed from type set within the limits of the United States, or from plates made therefrom." A refer-

Appendix V., p. 159.

ence to the words of the statute will show that this follows immediately upon the direction for delivery of "two copies of such *copyright book, map, chart, dramatic or musical composition, engraving, chromo, cut, print, or photograph.*" Is, then, a dramatic or musical composition, which in form would answer the description of "book" in the ordinary acceptation of the term, within the words of the proviso, so that the type must be set in the United States? It may be argued with some force that the contrast in the statute between "book" and "dramatic or musical composition" is more apparent than real; a work may be at the same time a dramatic piece for the purposes of the

Sec. 4952.
Sec. 4956.

principal section, and a book (if it is so in form) for the purposes of the proviso as to printing; it will be said that "dramatic composition" is mentioned separately in the principal section only because there may be plays which are not in book form, or even printed, but that those which are in book form

See Clark v. Bishop, 25 L. T. N. S. 911.

are not the less books because the composition has a histrionic flavour. If this be not so it will be said—you fall into this absurdity; you bring to the librarian a thing which persons endowed with ordinary faculties would call a "book," and on his objecting that as such it should have been printed in the United States, he is told: "You are the victim of an illusion, your senses deceive you, this is not a book and only looks like one; these boards cover a play, or at any rate something having a dramatic character; it may be a work in the nature of the "Théâtre impossible" of Edmond About, it may be a drawing-room charade for the use of children—all one; it is

a dramatic composition and may be printed anywhere. This would at
first sight seem a paradox only to be matched by Mr.
Wardle's definition of his sister: "She's a miss, and yet she   See "Bar-
ain't a miss." The thing is a book, and yet it is not a book.   ring Out,"
                                                                  by Miss
Notwithstanding, however, the seeming contradiction, it   Edge-
is probable that in the construction of the Act, "book" will   worth.
be confined to literary compositions, as opposed to dramatic
and musical ones. A reference to the sections of the Tariff Acts and a
comparison of other American statutes all lead to the conclusion that if the
question ever calls for decision in America, it will be held that no composition having a dramatic or musical character, though in
form a book, need be printed from the type set in the   5 & 6 Vic.
United States. This would not be inconsistent with the   ch. 45, sec. 2.
English doctrine which required a special interpretation clause in order
that a sheet of music should come within the definition of a book.

The clauses imposing penalties on infringement afford a strong argument
for confining the word "book" to literary matter; those clauses impose
separate penalties for violating the copyright in books on
the one hand and dramatic or musical compositions on the   Secs. 4964,
other; and the result of holding that "book" could include   4965.
such compositions would be that an infringer might incur double penalties,
which seems improbable in the last degree.

As a matter of fact Mr. Spofford, the present librarian of Congress,
receives copies of dramatic or musical compositions, though in book form,
wherever they may have been printed. The practice in America is to attach
more weight than in England to the procedure adopted by official function-
aries, and if the matter afterwards comes before the Courts on the action of
some person who has succeeded in passing the custom-house authorities or
the librarian, the maxim *potior est ratio possidentis* is often applied by the
judges; nor are there wanting cases in the American law reports where, in
a degree shocking to the traditions of an English lawyer, evidence of the
circumstances under which the statute was framed, or of amendments which
have been rejected, has been admitted as legitimate on the question of construction. Two senators (Messrs. Frye and Sherman) severally proposed
amendments to the Act of 1891, having for their effect the introduction of
the words "musical and dramatic compositions" into the proviso as to
printing, so as to exclude all doubt that such compositions must be printed
as the proviso directs. The fact that such amendments were lost goes far
to show that the intention of the legislature was to exempt all dramatic or
musical compositions from the proviso as to printing.

Importation of copyright is prohibited of copyright books . . . . or
lithographs or any plates thereof not made from type set, negatives or
drawings on stone made within the limits of the United   Sec. 4956.
States. This prohibition is subject to a number of exceptions,
of which the only important ones for the purposes of this work are: the case
of persons purchasing for use, and not for sale, subject to duty, not more
than two copies of any book; and the case of books in foreign languages
of which only translations in English are copyrighted, in which case the
originals may be imported. These exceptions are only important for
present purposes in the case of dramatic and musical compositions being
held to come within the definition "book" for certain purposes.

The combined effect of the proviso requiring two copies to be printed and the prohibition on importation is that *all* copies to be sold in America must be printed there.

The following four sections need not be noticed. There follows then an enactment imposing a penalty for the impression of an untrue notice upon any "book, map, chart, dramatic, or musical composition, print, cut, engraving, or photograph, or other article for which he has not obtained copyright. The notice which is here contemplated was one prescribed as a necessary condition precedent to an action for infringement.

Statute of 8th July, 1870, sec. 4962.

Under this section a notice must be inserted in the several copies of every published edition on the title page, or the page immediately following it, "if it *be book* (sic), or if a map, chart, musical composition" . . . . by inscribing on some portion of the front or face thereof the words

Act of June, 1874.

"entered according to act of Congress in the year   by A B in the office of the librarian of Congress at Washington," or "copyright 18—, by A B."

The sections above referred to which deal with penalties for violation deserve notice as bearing out the construction hereinbefore assigned to the term "book." Infringement of the title of a book is dealt

4064 & 4965.

with by the first of the two sections in question, which enacts that every person who without the consent in writing of the proprietor prints, publishes, dramatises, translates, or imports, or, knowing of the copyright, sells any copy of a *book*, shall forfeit every copy to the proprietor and pay damages. The second section in question relates to a map, chart, *dramatic or musical composition*, print, cut, engraving, or photograph, and to certain items not within the scope of this treatise. In this case the wrongful acts specified are, without consent in writing to engrave, print, publish, dramatise, translate, or import, or knowingly sell copies of the pirated article: the penalty is forfeiture to the proprietor of all plates and sheets either copied or printed, and payment of a dollar for every sheet found in his possession. The distinction between "book" on the one hand, and "dramatic or musical work" on the other, is considerably emphasised by the tenor of these two sections.

It remains to notice the liability to damages thrown upon any person

4967.

who shall print or publish any manuscript without consent of the author or proprietor.

The clause requiring printing on the spot has created considerable alarm among persons interested in the printing and analogous trades in England. It cannot be doubted that to some extent those trades will be affected; in what degree time alone can show. In many cases a double edition will be printed in America without stopping the machine; and the printed sheets only be brought here. In order to counteract the injurious effect of this clause, a deputation waited upon Sir Michael Hicks-Beach at the Board of Trade, and proposed the scheme of a Bill to be introduced by the Government under which an analogous provision to that relating to printing in the American Act would have been introduced into England, but the Board of Trade declined to entertain the proposal as being premature.

APPENDIX V.

The text of the New American Copyright Act is as follows :—

(*March 3rd*, 1891.) Be it enacted,—That section 4,952 of the Revised Statutes be and the same is hereby amended so as to read as follows :—" Section 4,952.—The author, inventor, designer, or proprietor of any book, map, chart, dramatic or musical composition, engraving, cut, print, or photographic negative thereof, or of a painting, drawing, chromo, statue, statuary, and of models or designs intended to be perfected as works of fine arts, and the executors, administrators, or assigns of any such person shall, upon complying with the provisions of this chapter, have the sole liberty of printing, reprinting, publishing, completing, copying, executing, finishing, and vending the same, and, in the case of dramatic composition, of publicly performing or representing it, or causing it to be performed or represented by others, and authors or their assigns shall have exclusive right to dramatise and translate any of their works for which copyright shall have been obtained under the laws of the United States."

Section 2.—That section 4,954 of the Revised Statutes be and the same is hereby amended so as to read as follows :—" Section 4,954.—The author, inventor, or designer, if he be still living, or his widow or children, if he be dead, shall have the same exclusive right continued for the further term of fourteen years, upon recording the title of the work or description of the article so secured a second time, and complying with all other regulations in regard to original copyright within six months before the expiration of the first term, and such person shall, within two months from the date of said renewal, cause a copy of the record thereof to be published in one or more newspapers printed in the United States for the space of four weeks."

Section 3.—That section 4,956 of the Revised Statutes of the United States be and the same is hereby amended so that it shall read as follows :—" Section 4,956.—No person shall be entitled to a copyright unless he shall, on or before the day of publication in this or any foreign country, deliver at the office of the Librarian of Congress, or deposit in the mail within the United States, addressed to the Librarian of Congress at Washington, district of Columbia, a printed copy of the title of the book, map, chart, dramatic or musical composition, engraving, cut, print, photograph or chromo, or a description of the painting, drawing, statue, statuary, or a model or design for a work of the fine arts, for which he desires a copyright, nor unless he shall also, not later than the day of the publication thereof in this or any foreign country, deliver at the office of the Librarian of Congress at Washington, district of Columbia, or deposit in the mail within the United States, addressed to the Librarian of Congress at Washington, district of Columbia, two copies of such copyright book, map, chart, dramatic or musical composition, engraving, chromo, cut, print, or photograph, or in case of a painting, drawing, statue, statuary, model, or design for a work of the fine arts, a photograph of the same ; provided that in case of a book, photograph, chromo, or lithograph, the two copies of the same required to be delivered or deposited as above shall be printed from type set within the limits of the United States, or from plates made therefrom, or from negatives or drawings on stone made within the limits of the United States, or from transfers made therefrom. During the existence of such copyright, the importation into the United States of any book, chromo, lithograph, or photograph so copyrighted, or any edition or editions thereof, or any plates of the same not made from type set, negatives, or drawings on stone made within the limits of the United States, shall be and it is hereby prohibited, except in the cases specified in paragraphs 512 to 516 inclusive in section two of the Act entitled ' An Act to reduce the revenue and equalise the duties on imports, and for other purposes,' approved October 1st, 1890 ; and except in the case of persons purchasing for use, and not for sale, who import subject to the duty thereon not more than two copies of such book at any one time ; and except in the case of newspapers and magazines not containing in whole or in part matter copyrighted under the provision of this Act, unauthorised by the author, which are hereby exempted from prohibition of importation ; provided, nevertheless, that in the cases of books in foreign languages of which only translations in English are copyrighted, the prohibition of importation shall apply only to the translation of the same, and the importation of the books in the original language shall be permitted."

Section 4.—That section 4,958 of the Revised Statutes be and the same is hereby amended so that it will read as follows:—"Section 4,958.—The Librarian of Congress shall receive, from the persons to whom the services designated are rendered, the following fees:—First, for recording the title or description of any copyright book or other article, 50c.; second, for every copy under seal of such record actually given to the person claiming the copyright or his assigns, 50c.: third, for recording and certifying an instrument of writing for the assignment of a copyright, $1; fourth, for every copy of an assignment, $1. All fees so received shall be paid into the Treasury of the United States, provided that the charge for recording the title or description of any article entered for copyright, the production of a person not a citizen or resident of the United States, shall be $1, to be paid as above into the Treasury of the United States to defray the expenses of the list of copyright articles, as hereinafter provided for. And it is hereby made the duty of the Librarian of Congress to furnish to the Secretary of the Treasury copies of the entries of titles of all books and other articles wherein the copyright has been completed by the deposit of two copies of such book, printed from type set within the limits of the United States; in accordance with the provisions of this Act, and by the deposit of two copies of such other article made or produced in the United States: and the Secretary of the Treasury is hereby directed to prepare and print, at intervals of not more than a week, catalogues of such title entries for distribution to the collectors of customs of the United States, and to the postmasters of all post-offices receiving foreign mails; and such weekly lists as they are issued shall be furnished to all parties desiring them at a sum not exceeding $5 per annum; and the Secretary and the Postmaster-General are hereby empowered and required to make and enforce such rules and regulations as shall prevent the importation into the United States, except upon the conditions above specified, of all articles prohibited by this Act."

Section 5.—That section 4,959 of the Revised Statutes be and the same is hereby amended so as to read as follows:—"Section 4,959.—The proprietor of every copyright book or other articles shall deliver at the office of the Librarian of Congress at Washington, district of Columbia, a copy of every subsequent edition wherein any substantial changes shall be made; provided, however, that the alterations, revisions, and additions made to books by foreign authors, heretofore published, of which new editions shall appear subsequently to the taking effect of this Act, shall be held and deemed capable of being copyrighted as above provided for in this Act, unless they form a part of the series in course of publication at the time this Act shall take effect."

Section 6.—That section 4,963 of the Revised Statutes be and the same is hereby amended so as to read as follows:—"Section 4,963.—Every person who shall insert or impress such notice, or words of the same purport, in or upon any book, map, chart, dramatic or musical composition, print, cut, engraving, or photograph, or other articles for which he has not obtained a copyright, shall be liable to a penalty of $100, recoverable one-half for the person who shall sue for such penalty and one-half for the use of the United States."

Section 7.—That section 4,964 of the Revised Statutes be and the same is hereby amended so as to be read as follows:—"Section 4,964.—Every person who, after the recording of the title of any book and the depositing of two copies of such book as provided by this Act, shall, contrary to the provisions of this Act, within the term limited, and without the consent of the proprietor of a copyright first obtained in writing, signed in the presence of two or more witnesses, print, publish, dramatise, translate, or import, or knowing the same to be so printed, published, dramatised, translated, or imported shall sell, or expose to sale, any copy of such book, shall forfeit every copy thereof to such proprietor, and shall also forfeit and pay such damages as may be recovered in a civil action by such proprietor in any Court of competent jurisdiction."

Section 8.—That section 4,965 of the Revised Statutes be and the same is hereby amended so as to read as follows:—"Section 4,965.—If any person after the recording of the title of any map, chart, dramatic or musical composition, print, cut, engraving or photograph, or chromo, or of the description of any painting, drawing, statue, statuary, or model or design intended to be perfected and executed as a work of the fine arts as provided by this Act, shall, within the term limited, contrary to the provisions of this Act, and without the consent of the proprietor of the copyright first obtained in writing, signed in the presence of two or more witnesses, engrave, etch, work, copy, print, publish, dramatise, translate, or import, either in whole or in part, or by varying the main design with intent to evade the law, or knowing the same to be so printed, published, dramatised, translated, or imported shall sell or expose to sale any copy of such map or other article as aforesaid, he shall forfeit to the proprietor all the plates on which the same shall be copied, and every sheet thereon either copied or printed, and shall further forfeit $1 for every sheet of the same found in his possession, either printed, copied, published, imported, or exposed for sale; and in case of a painting, statue, or statuary he shall forfeit $10 for every copy of the same in his possession or by him sold or exposed for sale, one-half thereof to the proprietor and the other half to the United States."

Section 9.—That section 4,967 of the Revised Statutes be and the same is hereby amended so as to read as follows :—" Section 4,967.—Every person who shall print or publish any manuscript whatever, without the consent of the author or proprietor first obtained, shall be liable to the author or proprietor for all damages occasioned by such injury."

Section 10.—That section 4,791 of the Revised Statutes be and the same is hereby repealed.

Section 11.—That for the purpose of this Act each volume of a book in two or more volumes, when such volumes are published separately, and the first one shall not have been issued before this Act shall take effect, and each number of a periodical shall be considered an independent publication subject to the form of copyrighting above.

Section 12.—That this Act shall go into effect on the 1st day of July, A.D. 1891.

Section 13.—That this Act shall only apply to a citizen or subject of a foreign State or nation when such foreign State or nation permits to citizens of the United States of America the benefit of copyright on substantially the same basis as its own citizens, or when such foreign State or nation is a party to an international agreement which provides for reciprocity in the granting of copyright, by the terms of which agreement the United States of America may at its pleasure become a party to such an agreement. The existence of either of the conditions aforesaid shall be determined by the President of the United States by proclamation made from time to time as the purposes of this Act may require.

(*July 1st.*) " Whereas it is provided by Section 13 of the Act of Congress of March 3, 1891, that the said Act shall only apply to a citizen or subject of a foreign State or nation when such foreign State or nation permits to citizens of the United States the benefit of copyright on substantially the same basis as to its own citizens or when such foreign State or nation is a party to an international agreement which provides for reciprocity in the granting of copyright, by the terms of which agreement the United States may, at their pleasure, become a party to such agreement, and whereas satisfactory official assurances have been given in Belgium, France, Great Britain, the British possessions, and Switzerland, that the law permits citizens of the United States the same benefit of copyright as to their own citizens ; now, therefore, I as President do declare and proclaim that the first conditions specified in the said Section 13 are now fulfilled in respect to the citizens and subjects of Belgium, France, Great Britain, and Switzerland.

APPENDIX VI.

(See p. 87.)

The sections in the Copyright Acts imposing registration are the following:—

By the Copyright Amendment Act it was enacted that "book" shall include "sheet of music," and that "dramatic piece" shall include "dramatic entertainment." Sections 6, 7, and 8 provide for the delivery of copies at the British Museum and Stationers' Hall. Section 11 provides for the keeping a book of registry at Stationers' Hall. Section 13 enacts that certain particulars may be entered, including the name and place of abode of the publisher. Section 20 provides that the provisions of the previous Act of William IV., and of the now reciting Act, shall apply to musical compositions . . . and that "the provisions hereinbefore enacted in respect of the property of such copyright, and of registering the same, shall apply to the liberty of representing or performing any dramatic piece or musical composition, as if the same were expressly re-enacted and applied" thereto. Section 24 enacts that "no proprietor of copyright . . . shall maintain any action or suit in respect of any infringement of such copyright unless he shall, before commencing his proceedings, have caused an entry to be made at Stationers' Hall pursuant to the Act." Nothing is to prejudice the remedies of the proprietor of performing right of a dramatic piece under the Act of William IV.

[margin: 5 & 6 Vict., c. 45.]
[margin: 3 & 4 Wm. IV., c. 15, supra p. 47. 5 & 6 Vict., c. 45.]
[margin: 3 Wm. IV., c. 15.]

According to the best opinion, the necessity for registration before suing applies to performance of a musical composition.

By the International Copyright Act, 1844, provision was made for granting by Order in Council copyright to foreigners, and "all enactments of the Copyright Amendment Act, and of any other Act for the time being in force with relation to copyright," are to apply to books to which such order shall extend, and "which shall have been registered as hereinafter is provided," except those relating to the delivery of copies.

[margin: 7 & 8 Vict., c. 12, secs. 2 & 3, supra p. 73.]

The registration clauses require the entry of particulars of items which are not identical with those prescribed by the Act of 1842; in particular no mention of the publisher or his abode need be made in registration under any of the *International Copyright Acts*. On these facts, it may be argued that the framer of the Act of 1886 has by inadvertence failed to exempt members of the federated countries from the necessity of registering under the Copyright Acts, and of entering the name and place of abode of the publisher. It is true that the section imposing upon foreigners the registration provisions of the *Copyright Amendment Act* is contained in one of the *International Copyright Acts*, and that the provisions of those latter Acts are not to apply (unless it is so provided by Order in Council), but the Act of 1886 (as was pointed out in the case below referred to) carefully separates the *International Copyright Acts* from the *Copyright Acts*, even to the extent of placing them in separate schedules; and the probability is that the framer of the Act of 1886 had not present to his mind the fact (which has apparently escaped the attention of text writers as well as legislators) that there is a difference between the forms of registration in the two classes of Acts, and that the exclusion of one class does not involve

[margin: 7 & 8 Vict., ch. 12, secs. 3 & 5.]

the abolition of the other ; had the point occurred to him he would unquestionably have excluded doubt by mentioning both.

In the case of Fishburn v. Hollingshead the question arose in respect of a painting exhibited by the defendants, and which was held to be a colourable imitation of the picture belonging to the plaintiffs.

<small>2 Ch. 1891.
371 25 & 26
Vict., ch. 68.</small>

The plaintiffs had purported to register under one of the Copyright Acts, but it was alleged by the defendants that the form of such registration was insufficient. The Court held in the result that the form of registration adopted was valid ; but as the necessity for any registration at all had been dealt with at great length in the argument, Mr. Justice Stirling delivered an elaborate judgment dealing with the point, although not calling for actual decision ; as, even assuming that registration was a condition precedent to suing, the plaintiffs were held to have complied with their obligation. The *International Copyright Act*, 1844, sec. 4, applies to foreign works of art "all the enactments of any Act for the time being in force with relation to the copyright here in any similar works of art," and the question of registration under 25 & 26 Vict., ch. 68, is identical with that under the *Copyright Amendment Act*, 1842 ; and the same arguments for and against the necessity for registration apply in both cases. The Court held that the necessity for registration under the *Copyright Acts* is not removed by sec. 4 of the Act of 1886. The learned judge considered that the legislature provided jealously that no author of a foreign work should be in a better position in this country than a British author.

The importance of this case is very great, for the public opinion is unquestionably against the necessity for registration in international cases, and the writers believe that the practice has been not to make any entry of foreign works, certainly the plaintiff in Moul v. Groenings (who represented French authors and composers collectively) had not been advised to register before suing ; but, as hereinbefore stated, there was no necessity for the Court to decide the point, as the plaintiff was defeated on another ground.

<small>Law Reports, 1891.</small>

The defendants in Fishburn v. Hollingshead afterwards accepted the judgment of Mr. Justice Stirling as final, and submitted to an injunction on that footing.

<small>2 Chancery.
5 & 6 Vict.,
c. 45.</small>

The result is that before suing in Great Britain for infringement of copyright in a musical or dramatic composition, or of performing right in a dramatic composition, it is prudent to register at Stationers' Hall under the Copyright Amendment Act, although the work may have been first published abroad, and is therefore one which depends for protection on the International Copyright Acts.

APPENDIX VII.

TERMS OF FOREIGN COPYRIGHT.

THE term of copyright is as follows in the countries signatories to the Berne Convention:—

SIGNATORIES TO THE BERNE CONVENTION.
- Spain—author's life, and 80 years after.
- Tunis—author's life, and 50 years after.
- Italy—author's life, and 40 years after. To be 80 years in any event.
- France—author's life, and fifty years after.
- Germany—author's life, and 30 years after.
- Switzerland—author's life, and 30 years after.
- Haiti—author's life, widow's life, children's lives, and 20 years after.
- Belgium—author's life, and 50 years after.

Mexico—in perpetuity.
Guatemala—in perpetuity.
Venezuela—in perpetuity.
Colombia—author's life, and 80 years after.
Ecuador—author's life, and 50 years after.
Norway—author's life, and 50 years after.
Peru—author's life, and 50 years after.
Russia—author's life, and 50 years after.
Austria—author's life, and 30 years after.
Brazil—author's life, and 10 years after.
Sweden—author's life, and 10 years after.
Roumania—author's life, and 10 years after.
Japan—author's life, and 5 years after.
South Africa—author's life, 50 years in any event.
Bolivia—author's life.
Denmark—50 years.
Holland—50 years.
America—28 years from recording the title with right to prolong for 14 years.

INDEX.

ABODE—
  Of proprietor of copyright to be registered, 49, 50

ACTIONS—
  Limitation of, 26

ACTS—
  Dramatic Copyright Act, 10 and foll.; Copyright Amendment Act, 11, and foll.; International Copyright Act, 72, and foll.; Colonial Copyright Act, 105, 106; Canadian Copyright Act, 106, and foll.; New American Copyright Act, 159

ADAPTATIONS—
  Of novels for stage, 14
  Of foreign dramatic works, 96, 97

AGREEMENTS—
  Forms of, Appendix III., 146

AMERICA—
  Copyright in, 154
  New Copyright Act, 159

ARTICLES—
  See Periodicals

ASSIGNEE—
  Of copyright, 42-46
  How differing from original proprietor, 48
  When liable to pay royalty, 153

ASSIGNMENT—
  By act of party, 40
  By operation of law, 40
  By implication, 41
  By intestacy, 40
  How differing from licence, 46
  Seal not necessary, 22
  Attestation not necessary, 22
  By entry at Stationers' Hall, 42
  Oral, not sufficient, 23

AUSTRALIA—
  See Colonial Copyright

AUSTRIA—
  See International Copyright

AUTHOR—
  Who is an, 12
  Joint authors, 12
  Arrangers of music, 12, 33
  Common law rights of, 2
  Consent of, to performance, 23
  Rights of, before publication, 10
  Rights of, on publication, 10
  Statutory rights of, 3

BANKRUPTCY—
  Effect of, on authors' rights, 40

BARS—
  Of music, how many to constitute piracy, 65

BELGIUM—
  See International Copyright

BERNE CONVENTION—
 Colonies, how far affected, 100
 Countries parties to, 74
 Dramatic works under, 79
 Musical works under, 79
 Duration of, 76
 Interpretation clause, 77
 Ratification of, 76
 Retrospective operation, 81
 Terms of copyright, under, 80
 Translations, 91

BLASPHEMOUS WORK—
 No copyright in, 19

BODLEIAN LIBRARY—
 See Deposit of Copies, 55

BONA-FIDES—
 No defence to action for infringement, 67

BOOK—
 What is a, 28

BRITISH DOMINIONS—
 Residence in, affecting copyright, 59, 60

BRITISH MUSEUM—
 See Deposit of Copies, 55
 How differing from other libraries, 56

BRITISH POSSESSIONS—
 What are, 100
 Importance of definition, 100
 Copyright in, 100, and foll.

CANADA—
 Copyright in, 106, and foll.

CASES CITED—
 See Case Index

COLONIAL COPYRIGHT—
 Duration of, 104, 105, 106
 Effect of Berne Convention on, 101

COMMISSION—
 Royal, on copyright, 14, 17

COMMISSIONERS OF CUSTOMS—
 Lists of copyright works to be sent to, 70

COMPOSITION—
 Dramatic, what is a, 18

CONGRESS—
 Librarian of, Appendix IV. V.

CONSENT—
 For performance, 23
 What amounts to, 23

*CONVENTIONS—*6, 7, 8

COPIES—
 Deposit of, 55, 56
 Importation of, 69
 Action for delivery up of, 69

COPYRIGHT—
 Nature of, 10
 Extent, 11
 Duration, 11, 35
 At common law, 10
 By statute, 10
 In titles, 30, 31
 In arrangements of music, 33
 Magazine articles, 38, 39
 New editions, 54, 55
 Novels, 14, and foll.

COSTS—
 Double, repealed, 26

COUNCIL—
 Orders in, 6, and *passim*.

DAMAGES—
  For unlawful multiplication of copies, 58, 59, 68
  For unauthorised performance, 60, 61
  For unlawful importation, 69

DELIVERY UP—
  Of pirated copies, 69

DEPOSIT—
  Of copies at libraries, 55, 56
  Neglect to, no bar to action, 57

DOUBLE COSTS—
  Provision for, repealed, 26

DRAMATIC COMPOSITIONS—18
  Copyright proper in, 28
  Performing rights in, 28
  How differing from musical, 64
  Representation of, 44, 60
  Publication of, 4, 87

DRAMATIC ENTERTAINMENT—
  What is a, 18
  Place of, 19

DRAMATIC PIECE—
  To include musical entertainment, 28

DRAMATIZATION—
  Of works not dramatic, 14-17
  How far lawful, 14-17
  How far unlawful, 14-17

DURATION OF COPYRIGHT—
  Home, 35-38
  Foreign, 164
  Colonial, 104

EDITIONS, NEW—
  What are, 55
  Registration of, 54

ENTRY—
  At Stationers' Hall, 42
  Forms of, 42, 43
  Condition precedent to suing, 47
  Errors in, 50
  Particulars in, 50-55

FEES FOR REGISTRATION—
  42, 43

FOREIGN AUTHORS—
  Publishing in the United Kingdom, 29
  Resident out of the United Kingdom, 29

FOREIGN COPYRIGHT—
  Terms of, 164

FORFEITURE—
  Of pirated copies, 69

FRANCE—
  See International Copyright

GERMANY—
  See International Copyright

GRATUITOUS DISTRIBUTION—
  Equivalent to publication, 58

HAITI—
  See International Copyright

IMMORAL WORKS—
  No copyright in, 19

IMPORTATION UNLAWFUL—
  Action for damages, 68
  For penalties, 69
  For copies, 69

IMPORTER, WRONGFUL—
  Liability of, 58

INFRINGEMENT—
  Of copyright proper, 57-60
  Of performing rights, 60-64
  Remedies for 68-70

INJUNCTION—
  No bar to other remedies, 71

INTERNATIONAL COPY-RIGHT—
  Conventions regarding, 6, 8, 73
  Early legislation, 6
  Registration for purposes of, 99
  Retrospective operation, 81
  Publication of dramatic works, 87
  Representation of dramatic works, 87
  Translations, 91
  Country of origin, 102

INTESTACY—
  Devolution of copyright on, 40

ITALY—
  See International Copyright

JOINT AUTHORS—
  What are, 12

KNOWLEDGE—
  Where essential in piracy, 60

LIBRARIES—
  Deposit of copies at, 55, 56
  British Museum, 56
  Bodleian, Oxford, 56
  Public Library, Cambridge, 56

LICENCE—
  For performance to be in writing, 23
  Its difference from assignment, 46

LIMITATION—
  Of actions, 26

LISTS OF COPYRIGHT WORKS—
  For Commissioners of Customs, 70

LITERARY LARCENY—64–67

MANUSCRIPTS—
  Rights in, 10
  On bankruptcy, 40

MUSICAL COMPOSITIONS—
  Re-arrangements, 12
  Adaptation of new words, 31, 32
  Performance of, 60, 61
  Reservation of performing rights, 62
  How differing from dramatic, 64

MUSICAL ENTERTAINMENT—
  What is a, 61, 62

NAME—
  Of proprietor to be registered, 49

NOVELS—
  Dramatization of, 14–17
  Representation of drama, 14–17
  Publication of copies, 14–17

ORDERS IN COUNCIL—
  See International Copyright

ORIGIN—
  Registration in country of, 102

PENALTIES—
  For non-delivery of copies, 56, 57
  For unlawful importation, 69
  For wrongful performance, 22, 24, 45

PERFORMANCE—
  Consent to, 23
  Reservation of right in musical compositions, 62, 79
  Responsibility for, 24
  Unlawful, what is, 62
  Wrongful, penalty for, 22, 24

PERFORMING RIGHTS—
  Difference from copyright proper, 28

INDEX. 169

PERIODICALS—
Articles in, 37, 48
Date of publication of, 54

PIANOFORTE ARRANGE-
MENTS—
Copyright in, 33

PIRACY—
See Infringement

PRINTER—
His liability for piracy, 58

PROPRIETOR—
When he must register, 47
When not, 47, 48

PUBLICATION—
Effect of, 10
Date of, its importance, 36
Simultaneous home and foreign, 79, 80
Representation equivalent to, 89, 90
Place of, to be registered, 49
Payment not essential to, 58
Printing not essential to, 58
Date of, to be registered, 51

PUBLISHER—
Who is a, 51, 53
First publisher to be registered, 51
Name and abode to be registered, 54
Specimen agreements with, Appendix III.
How affected by Berne Convention, 75, 79, 81

REGISTRATION—
Assignment by, 42
Precedent to suing, 47
Omission to register, 47
False entry, 50
Formalities of, 49, 51

REGISTRATION (Continued)—
For International copyright, 99 et seq.

REMEDIES—
By action for damages, 68
By action for penalties, 69
By action for delivery of copies, 69
By injunction, 71

REPRESENTATION—
Right of, differs from copyright, 28
Effect of, on performing rights, 34
Effect of, on copyright proper, 35
Public distinct from private, 20, 21
Remedies for unlawful, 68
Under Berne Convention, 92, 93

REPRINTS—55

RESERVATION—
Of performing rights, to be notified, 62

RESIDENCE—
Of proprietor to be registered, 49, 50

ROYALTIES—
Whether a charge on copyright, 153

RUSSIA—
No copyright with, 33

SEDITIOUS WORKS—
No copyright in, 19

SEPARATE PUBLICATION—
Of articles in periodicals, 37, 38

SIMULTANEOUS PUBLICA-
TION—
At home and abroad, 79, 80

SONGS—
New words to old airs, 31, 32

SPAIN—
  See International Copyright
SUBSTANTIAL PART—
  Piracy must be of a, 65
SWITZERLAND—
  See International Copyright
TITLES—
  Copyright in, 31
TRANSLATIONS—
  Author's right to prevent, 91
  Copyright in authorised, 91
  Independent works, 93, 95
  When public property, 91
  Unauthorised, 33, 95
TUNIS—
  See International Copyright
UNITED KINGDOM—
  Publication in, 29
  Its necessity for copyright, 29
  How modified, 30

UNITED STATES—
  See American Copyright, 154
UNPUBLISHED WORKS—
  Rights in, 10, 40
WORKS REFERRED TO—
  "Colleen Bawn," 4, 34, 88
  "Elfin Waltzer," 34
  "Enoch Arden," 18
  "Father O'Flynn," 32
  "Faust," 7
  "Frou Frou," 96
  "Little Lord Fauntleroy," 14, 15
  "Low-backed Car," 31
  "Northern Farmer," 18
  "Oberon," 67
  "Pestal," 31
  "Rienzi," 94
  "Shaughraun," 38, 90
  "Ship on Fire," 19
  "Vert-Vert," 50, 51
  "Will-o'-the-Wisp," 61

ABBREVIATIONS.

GENERAL.

Art.—Article.
Ann.—Anne.
c. ⎫
cap. ⎬ Chapter.
ch. ⎭
Car. II.—Charles II.
Ex p. ⎫
 or ⎬ Ex parte.
Ex pte. ⎭
Geo. III.—George III.
L.S.—Locus sigilli.

M.R.—Master of the Rolls.
s. ⎫
sec. ⎬ Section.
sect. ⎭
s.s. ⎫
sub-sec. ⎬ Sub-section.
V.C.—Vice-Chancellor.
Vict.—Victoria.
Will. IV. ⎫
Wm. IV. ⎬ William IV.

ABBREVIATIONS USED IN REFERENCE TO LAW REPORTS.

A. & E.—Adolphus & Ellis's Reports.
App. C. or App. Cas.—Law Reports, Appeal Cases.
B. & C. ⎫
 or ⎬ Barnwall & Cresswell's Reports.
Barn. & Cres. ⎭
Bing.—Bingham's Reports.
Bing. N.C.—Bingham's New Cases.
Blatch — Blatch's American Reports.
Bos. & Pul.—Bosanquet & Puller's Reports.
Bro. Parl. Cas. ⎫ Brown's Cases in
Bro. P.C.   ⎬ Parliament.
Burr.—Burrows' Reports.
C. & K. ⎫
 or ⎪
Car. & Kir. ⎬ Carrington & Kirwan's Reports.
 or ⎪
Car. & Kirw. ⎭

C.B.—Common Bench Reports, or Manning, Grainger, & Scott's Reports.
C.B.N.S.—Common Bench Reports, New Series.
C.D. ⎫
Ch.D. ⎪
 or ⎬ Law Reports, Chancery Division.
Ch.Div. ⎭
C.P.—Common Pleas.
C.P.D.—Law Reports, Common Pleas Division.
C. & P. ⎫
 or ⎬ Carrington & Payne's Reports.
Car. & P. ⎭
D.M. & G. ⎫ De Gex, Macnagh-
De Gex, Mac. ⎬ ten & Gordon's
& Gordon ⎭ Reports.
Eng. & Ir. App.—Law Reports, House of Lords (English and Irish Appeals).

ABBREVIATIONS.

Eq.—Law Reports, Equity.
Esp.—Espinasse's Reports.
H. & C.—Hurlstone & Coltman's Reports.
H. & N.—Hurlstone & Norman's Reports.
H.L.C. or H.L. Cas. or H.L. Rep.} Clark & Finnelly's House of Lords Reports.
H. & M. or Hem. & M. or Hem. & Mil.} Hemming & Miller's Reports.
J. & H. or John. & H.} Johnson & Hemming's Reports.
Jur.—Jurist Reports.
Jur. N.S.—Jurist, New Series.
K. & J. or Kay & J.} Kay & Johnson's Reports.
L.R.—Law Reports.
L.J.—*Law Journal.*
L.J.Ch.—*Law Journal, Chancery.*

L.T.—*The Law Times.*
L.T.N.S.—*Law Times, New Series.*
Mac. & G. or Mac. & Gor.} Macnaghten & Gordon's Reports.
Q.B.—Adolphus & Ellis, Queen's Bench Reports, New Series.
Q.B.D.—Law Reports, Queen's Bench Division.
Sol.J.—*Solicitors' Journal.*
Stra. or Strange} Strange's Reports.
T.R.—Term Reports (Durnford & East).
Times—*Times* Law Reports.
T.R.—Term Reports.
Ves. Sen.—Vesey's Sen. Reports.
Ves. or Ves. Jun.} Vesey's Jun. Reports.
W.N.—*Weekly Notes.*
W.R.—*Weekly Reporter.*
Y. & C.—Younge & Collyer's Reports.

CASE INDEX.

Adams v. Batley, 25
Attwill v. Ferrett, 12, 33

Boucicault v. Chatterton, 34, 90
Boucicault v. Delafield, 34, 78, 87, 88, 90
Boucicault v. Hart, 156
Bradbury v. Beeton, 30
British Museum v. Payne, 57

Cary v. Kearsley, 67
Chappell v. Boosey, 28, 35
Chappell v. Davidson, 51
Chatterton v. Cave, 18, 23, 65, 67
Clarke v. Bishop, 156
Clementi v. Walker, 34
Cocks v. Purday, 34, 79
Cole v. Francis, 25
Coleman v. Wathen, 34
Collingridge v. Emmott, 51
Cooper v. Whittingham, 60, 69, 71
Coote v. Judd, 52
Cumberland v. Copeland, 22
Cumberland v. Planché, 44

D'Almaine v. Boosey, 33, 65, 66, 67
Dicks v. Yates, 22, 30, 54, 64
Donaldson v. Beckett, 3, 88
Duck v. Bates, 20, 62

Eaton v. Lake, 23
Emerson v. Davies, 33

Farina v. Silverlock, 95
Fairlie v. Boosey, 50
Fishburn v. Hollinghead, 86, 163

Gartside v. Silkstone Co., 80
Gounod v. Wood, 30
Guichard v. Mori, 34, 72

Hatton v. Kean, 41
Hutchins v. Romer, 45

Jefferys v. Boosey, 10, 15, 29, 44

Lacey v. Toole, 41
Layland v. Stewart, 22
Leader v. Purday, 12, 31
Leader v. Strange, 60
Lee v. Simpson, 18
Levey v. Rutley, 13
London Printing Alliance v. Cox, 47
Longman v. Trip, 40
Low v. Routledge, 50, 54, 57
Lover v. Davidson, 31
Lyons v. Knowles, 25

Marsh v. Conquest, 22, 25, 48
Mathieson v. Harrod, 51
Maxwell v. Hogg, 30
Mayhew v. Maxwell, 37
Morton v. Copeland, 24
Moul v. Groenings, 84, 85
Murray v. Maxwell, 48

Nottage v. Jackson, 54
Novello v. Sudlow, 58

Planché v. Braham, 23, 65, 67
Powell v. Head, 24
Prince Albert v. Strange, 10

Reade v. Bentley, 1, 46, 55, 79
Reade v. Conquest, 14
Richardson v. Gilbert, 38, 41
Routledge v. Low, 29, 79
Russell v. Briant, 24
Russell v. Smith, 18, 19

Shelley v. Bethell, 21
Shepherd v. Conquest, 13, 23
Smiles v. Bedford, 112
Stockdale v. Onwhyn, 30
Sweet v. Benning, 42

Taylor v. Neville, 46
Thomas v. Turner, 54
Trade Auxiliary Co. v. Middlesborough, 37

Walcot v. Walker, 19
Wall v. Gordon, 156
Wall v. Taylor, 61
Walter v. Howe, 41
Warne v. Lawrence, 50, 80
Warne v. Seebohn, 12, 14, 17, 30, 32
Weldon v. Dicks, 30, 47, 51, 52
Werdeman v. Société Générale d'Électricité, 153
Wood v. Boosey, 12, 33
Wood v. Chart, 95, 96, 97

THE END.

Selections from Cassell & Company's Publications.

Illustrated, Fine-Art, and other Volumes.

Abbeys and Churches of England and Wales, The: Descriptive, Historical, Pictorial. Two Series. 21s. each.
Adventure, The World of. Fully Illustrated. Complete in Three Vols. 9s each.
American Library of Fiction. Crown 8vo, cloth, 3s. 6d. each.
    A Latin-Quarter Courtship. By Henry Harland (Sidney Luska).
    "89." By Edgar Henry.
    Kamel the Scout. By Sylvanus Cobb, Junr.
    Grandison Mather. By Henry Harland (Sidney Luska).
Anglomaniacs, The: A Story of New York Life of To-day. By Mrs. BURTON HARRISON. 3s. 6d.
Arabian Nights Entertainments, Cassell's Pictorial. 10s. 6d.
Architectural Drawing. By PHENÉ SPIERS. Illustrated. 10s. 6d.
Art, The Magazine of. Yearly Vol. With 12 Photogravures, Etchings, &c., and several hundred choice Engravings. 16s.
Artistic Anatomy. By Prof. M. DUVAL. Translated by F. E. FENTON. 5s.
Bashkirtseff, Marie, The Journal of. *Cheap Edition.* 7s. 6d. *Library Edition,* in Two Vols. 24s.
Bashkirtseff, Marie, The Letters of. Translated by MARY J. SERRANO. 7s. 6d.
Birds' Nests, Eggs, and Egg-Collecting. By R. KEARTON. Illustrated with 16 Coloured Plates. 5s.
Black America. A Study of the Ex-slave and his late Master. By W. LAIRD CLOWES. 6s.
Black Arrow, The. A Tale of the Two Roses. By R. L. STEVENSON. Illustrated. 3s. 6d.
British Ballads. With 275 Original Illustrations. In Two Vols. 15s.
British Battles on Land and Sea. By JAMES GRANT. With about 600 Illustrations. Three Vols., 4to, £1 7s.; *Library Edition,* £1 10s.
British Battles, Recent. Illustrated. 4to, 9s.; *Library Edition,* 10s.
Browning, An Introduction to the Study of. By A. SYMONS. 2s. 6d.
Bunyan's Pilgrim's Progress and The Holy War, Cassell's Illustrated Edition of. With 200 Original Illustrations. Cloth, 16s.
Butterflies and Moths, European. With 61 Coloured Plates. 35s.
Canaries and Cage-Birds, The Illustrated Book of. With 56 Facsimile Coloured Plates, 35s. Half-morocco, £2 5s.
Cassell's Family Magazine. Yearly Vol. Illustrated. 9s.
Cathedrals, Abbeys, and Churches of England and Wales. Descriptive, Historical, Pictorial. *Popular Edition.* Two Vols. 25s.
Celebrities of the Century. *Cheap Edition.* 10s. 6d.
Choice Dishes at Small Cost. By A. G. PAYNE. 1s.
Cities of the World. Four Vols. Illustrated. 7s. 6d. each.
Civil Service, Guide to Employment in the. 3s. 6d.
Civil Service.—Guide to Female Employment in Government Offices. 1s.
Climate and Health Resorts. By Dr. BURNEY YEO. *New and Cheaper Edition.* 7s. 6d.
Clinical Manuals for Practitioners and Students of Medicine. A List of Volumes forwarded post free on application to the Publishers.
Clothing, The Influence of, on Health. By F. TREVES, F.R.C.S. 2s.
Colonist's Medical Handbook, The. By E. A. BARTON, M.R.C.S. 2s. 6d.
Colour. By Prof. A. H. CHURCH. With Coloured Plates. 3s. 6d.
Commerce, The Year-Book of. Third Year's Issue. 5s.
Commercial Botany of the Nineteenth Century. By J. R. JACKSON, A.L.S. Cloth gilt, 3s. 6d.
Conning Tower, In a. By H. O. ARNOLD-FORSTER. 1s.
Cookery, A Year's. By PHYLLIS BROWNE. *New and Enlarged Edition.* 3s. 6d.

5 G. 9.91

Cookery, Cassell's Dictionary of. Containing about Nine Thousand Recipes, 7s. 6d. ; Roxburgh, 10s. 6d.
Cookery, Cassell's Popular. With Four Coloured Plates. Cloth gilt, 2s.
Cookery, Cassell's Shilling. 384 pages, limp cloth, 1s.
Cookery, Vegetarian. By A. G. PAYNE. 1s. 6d.
Cooking by Gas, The Art of. By MARIE J. SUGG. Illustrated. Cloth, 3s. 6d.
Copyright, The Law of Musical and Dramatic. By EDWARD CUTLER, THOMAS EUSTACE SMITH, and FREDERIC E. WEATHERLY, Esquires, Barristers-at-Law. 3s. 6d.
Countries of the World, The. By ROBERT BROWN, M.A., Ph.D., &c. Complete in Six Vols., with about 750 Illustrations. 4to, 7s. 6d. each.
Cromwell, Oliver. By J. ALLANSON PICTON, M.P. 5s.
Culmshire Folk. By the Author of "John Orlebar," &c. 3s. 6d.
Cyclopædia, Cassell's Concise. Brought down to the latest date. With about 600 Illustrations. *Cheap Edition*. 7s. 6d.
Cyclopædia, Cassell's Miniature. Containing 30,000 subjects. 3s. 6d.
Dairy Farming. By Prof. J. P. SHELDON. With 25 Coloured Plates. 21s.
David Todd. By DAVID MACLURE. 5s.
Dickens, Character Sketches from. FIRST, SECOND, and THIRD SERIES. With Six Original Drawings in each by F. BARNARD. 21s. each
Disraeli, Benjamin, Personal Reminiscences of. By HENRY LAKE. 3s. 6d.
Disraeli in Outline. By F. CARROLL BREWSTER, LL.D. 7s. 6d.
Dog, Illustrated Book of the. By VERO SHAW, B.A. With 28 Coloured Plates. Cloth bevelled, 35s. ; half-morocco, 45s.
Dog, The. By IDSTONE. Illustrated. 2s. 6d.
Domestic Dictionary, The. Illustrated. Cloth, 7s. 6d.
Doré Gallery, The. With 250 Illustrations by DORÉ. 4to, 42s.
Doré's Dante's Inferno. Illustrated by GUSTAVE DORÉ. 21s.
Doré's Milton's Paradise Lost. Illustrated by DORÉ. 4to, 21s.
Dr. Dumány's Wife. A Novel. By MAURUS JÓKAI. Translated from the Hungarian by F. STEINITZ. 7s. 6d. net.
Earth, Our, and its Story. By Dr. ROBERT BROWN, F.L.S. With Coloured Plates and numerous Wood Engravings. Three Vols. 9s. each.
Edinburgh, Old and New. With 600 Illustrations. Three Vols. 9s. each.
Egypt: Descriptive, Historical, and Picturesque. By Prof. G. EBERS. With 800 Original Engravings. *Popular Edition*. In Two Vols. 42s.
Electricity in the Service of Man. With nearly 850 Illustrations. *Cheap Edition*. 9s.
Electricity, Age of. By PARK BENJAMIN, Ph.D. 7s. 6d.
Electricity, Practical. By Prof. W. E. AYRTON. 7s. 6d.
Employment for Boys on Leaving School, Guide to. By W. S. Beard, F.R.G.S. 1s. 6d.
Encyclopædic Dictionary, The. Complete in Fourteen Divisional Vols., 10s. 6d. each ; or Seven Vols., half-morocco, 21s. each ; half-russia, 25s.
England, Cassell's Illustrated History of. With 2,000 Illustrations. Ten Vols., 4to, 9s. each. *Revised Edition*. Vols. I., II., III., and IV. 9s. each.
English Dictionary, Cassell's. Giving definitions of more than 100,000 words and phrases. 7s. 6d.
English History, The Dictionary of. *Cheap Edition*. 10s. 6d.
English Literature, Dictionary of. By W. DAVENPORT ADAMS. *Cheap Edition*, 7s. 6d. ; Roxburgh, 10s. 6d.

Selections from Cassell & Company's Publications.

English Literature, Library of. By Prof. HENRY MORLEY.
    VOL. I.—SHORTER ENGLISH POEMS. 7s. 6d.
    VOL. II.—ILLUSTRATIONS OF ENGLISH RELIGION. 7s. 6d.
    VOL. III.—ENGLISH PLAYS. 7s. 6d.
    VOL. IV.—SHORTER WORKS IN ENGLISH PROSE. 7s. 6d.
    VOL. V.—SKETCHES OF LONGER WORKS IN ENGLISH VERSE AND PROSE. 7s. 6d.
English Literature, Morley's First Sketch of. *Revised Edition*, 7s. 6d.
English Literature, The Story of. By ANNA BUCKLAND. 3s. 6d.
English Writers. By Prof. HENRY MORLEY. Vols. I. to VIII. 5s. each.
Æsop's Fables. Illustrated by ERNEST GRISET. Cloth, 3s. 6d.
Etiquette of Good Society. 1s.; cloth, 1s. 6d.
Eye, Ear, and Throat, The Management of the. 3s. 6d.
Faith Doctor, The. A Novel. By EDWARD EGGLESTON. 7s. 6d. net.
Family Physician, The. By Eminent PHYSICIANS and SURGEONS. *New and Revised Edition.* Cloth, 21s.; Roxburgh, 25s.
Father Stafford. A Novel. By ANTHONY HOPE. 6s.
Fenn, G. Manville, Works by. Boards, 2s. each; cloth, 2s. 6d. each.
POVERTY CORNER. | DUTCH THE DIVER. Boards only.
MY PATIENTS. Being the Notes of a Navy Surgeon. | THE VICAR'S PEOPLE. Cloth only.
    THE PARSON O' DUMFORD. Boards only.
Field Naturalist's Handbook, The. By the Rev. J. G. WOOD and Rev. THEODORE WOOD. 5s.
Figuier's Popular Scientific Works. With Several Hundred Illustrations in each. 3s. 6d. each.
    THE HUMAN RACE. | MAMMALIA. | OCEAN WORLD.
    WORLD BEFORE THE DELUGE. Revised.
Flora's Feast. A Masque of Flowers. Penned and Pictured by WALTER CRANE. With 40 Pages in Colours. 5s.
Flower de Hundred, The Story of a Virginia Plantation. By Mrs. BURTON HARRISON, Author of the "Anglomaniacs," &c. 3s. 6d.
Flower Painting in Water Colours. With Coloured Plates. First and Second Series. 5s. each.
Flower Painting, Elementary. With Eight Coloured Plates. 3s.
Flowers, and How to Paint Them. By MAUD NAFTEL. With Coloured Plates. 5s.
Fossil Reptiles, A History of British. By Sir RICHARD OWEN, K.C.B., F.R.S., &c. With 268 Plates. In Four Vols., £12 12s.
Four Years in Parliament with Hard Labour. By C. W. RADCLIFFE COOKE, M.P. *Third Edition.* 1s.
France as It Is. By ANDRÉ LEBON and PAUL PELET. With Three Maps. Crown 8vo, cloth, 7s. 6d.
Garden Flowers, Familiar. By SHIRLEY HIBBERD. With Coloured Plates by F. E. HULME, F.L.S. Complete in Five Series. 12s. 6d. each.
Gardening, Cassell's Popular. Illustrated. Four Vols. 5s. each.
Geometrical Drawing for Army Candidates. By H. T. LILLEY, M.A. 2s.
Geometry, First Elements of Experimental. By PAUL BERT. 1s. 6d.
Geometry, Practical Solid. By MAJOR ROSS. 2s.
Gilbert, Elizabeth, and her Work for the Blind. By FRANCES MARTIN. 2s. 6d.
Gleanings from Popular Authors. Two Vols. With Original Illustrations. 4to, 9s. each. Two Vols. in One, 15s.
Gulliver's Travels. With 88 Engravings by MORTEN. *Cheap Edition.* Cloth, 3s. 6d.; cloth gilt, 5s.
Gun and its Development, The. By W. W. GREENER. With 500 Illustrations. 10s. 6d.
Guns, Modern Shot. By W. W. GREENER. Illustrated. 5s.
Health at School. By CLEMENT DUKES, M.D., B.S. 7s. 6d.
Health, The Book of. By Eminent Physicians and Surgeons. 21s.
Health, The Influence of Clothing on. By F. TREVES, F.R.G.S. 2s.

Selections from Cassell & Company's Publications.

Heavens, The Story of the. By Sir ROBERT STAWELL BALL, LL.D., F.R.S., F.R.A.S. With Coloured Plates. *Popular Edition.* 12s. 6d.
Heroes of Britain in Peace and War. With 300 Original Illustrations. *Cheap Edition.* Vol. I. 3s. 6d.
Holiday Studies of Wordsworth. By Rev. F. A. MALLESON, M.A. 5s.
Horse, The Book of the. By SAMUEL SIDNEY. With 28 Fac-simile Coloured Plates. *Enlarged Edition.* Demy 4to, 35s.; half-morocco, 45s.
Houghton, Lord: The Life, Letters, and Friendships of Richard Monckton Milnes, First Lord Houghton. By T. WEMYSS REID. In Two Vols., with Two Portraits. 32s.
Household, Cassell's Book of the. Complete in Four Vols. 5s. each.
How Women may Earn a Living. By MERCY GROGAN. 6d.
Hygiene and Public Health. By B. ARTHUR WHITELEGGE, M.D. 7s. 6d.
India, Cassell's History of. By JAMES GRANT. With about 400 Illustrations. Library binding. One Vol. 15s.
In-door Amusements, Card Games, and Fireside Fun, Cassell's Book of. *Cheap Edition.* 2s.
Irish Union, The; Before and After. By A. K. CONNELL, M.A. 2s. 6d.
Italy from the Fall of Napoleon I. in 1815 to 1890. By J. W. PROBYN. *New and Cheaper Edition.* 3s. 6d.
"Japanese" Library of Popular Works, Cassell's. Consisting of Twelve Popular Works, printed on thin paper. 1s. 3d. each net.
    Handy Andy.—Oliver Twist.—Ivanhoe.—Ingoldsby Legends.—The Last of the Mohicans.—The Last Days of Pompeii—The Yellowplush Papers.—The Last Days of Palmyra—Jack Hinton, the Guardsman.—Selections from Hood's Works.—American Humour.—The Tower of London.

John Orlebar, Clk. By the Author of "Culmshire Folk." 2s.
John Parmelee's Curse. By JULIAN HAWTHORNE. 2s. 6d.
Kennel Guide, The Practical. By Dr. GORDON STABLES. 1s.
Khiva, A Ride to. By Col. FRED. BURNABY. 1s. 6d.
Kidnapped. By R. L. STEVENSON. Illustrated. 3s. 6d.
King Solomon's Mines. By H. RIDER HAGGARD. Illustrated. 3s. 6d.
Ladies' Physician, The. By a London Physician. 6s.
Lake Dwellings of Europe. By ROBERT MUNRO, M.D., M.A. Cloth, 31s. 6d.; Roxburgh, £2 2s.
Law, How to Avoid. By A. J. WILLIAMS, M.P. 1s. *Cheap Edition.*
Legends for Lionel. By WALTER CRANE. Coloured Illustrations. 5s.
Letts's Diaries and other Time-saving Publications published exclusively by CASSELL & COMPANY. (*A list free on application.*)
Life Assurance, Medical Handbook of. 7s. 6d.
Little Minister, The. By J. M. BARRIE. Three Vols. 31s. 6d.
Loans Manual. By CHARLES P. COTTON. 5s.
Local Government in England and Germany. By the Right Hon. Sir ROBERT MORIER, G.C.B., &c. 1s.
Local Option in Norway. By THOMAS M. WILSON, C.E. 1s.
Locomotive Engine, The Biography of a. By HENRY FRITH. 5s.
London, Greater. By EDWARD WALFORD. Two Vols. With about 400 Illustrations. 9s. each.
London, Old and New. Six Vols., each containing about 200 Illustrations and Maps. Cloth, 9s. each.
London Street Arabs. By Mrs. H. M. STANLEY (DOROTHY TENNANT). A Collection of Pictures. Descriptive Text by the Artist. 5s.
Master of Ballantrae, The. By R. L. STEVENSON. Illustrated. 3s. 6d.
Mathew, Father, His Life and Times. By F. J. MATHEW, a Grand-nephew. 2s. 6d.
Mechanics, The Practical Dictionary of. Containing 15,000 Drawings. Four Vols. 21s. each.
Medicine, Manuals for Students of. (*A List forwarded post free.*)
Metropolitan Year-Book, The, for 1892. Paper, 1s.; cloth, 2s.

Selections from Cassell & Company's Publications.

Metzerott, Shoemaker. Cr. 8vo, 5s.
Modern Europe, A History of. By C. A. FYFFE, M.A. Complete in Three Vols. 12s. each.
Music, Illustrated History of. By EMIL NAUMANN. Edited by the Rev. Sir F. A. GORE OUSELEY, Bart. Illustrated. Two Vols. 31s. 6d.
National Library, Cassell's. In Volumes. Paper covers, 3d.; cloth, 6d. *(A Complete List of the Volumes post free on application.)*
Natural History, Cassell's Concise. By E. PERCEVAL WRIGHT, M.A., M.D., F.L.S. With several Hundred Illustrations. 7s. 6d.
Natural History, Cassell's New. Edited by Prof. P. MARTIN DUNCAN, M.B., F.R.S., F.G.S. Complete in Six Vols. With about 2,000 Illustrations. Cloth, 9s. each.
Nature's Wonder Workers. By KATE R. LOVELL. Illustrated. 5s.
Naval War, The Last Great. By A. NELSON SEAFORTH. One Vol., with Maps and Plans. 2s.
Navy, Royal, All About The. By W. LAIRD CLOWES. Illustrated. 1s.
Nelson, The Life of. By ROBERT SOUTHEY. Illustrated with Eight Plates. 3s. 6d. An Edition of Southey's "Nelson" is published as a Volume of the National Library, price 3d. Cloth, 6d.
Nursing for the Home and for the Hospital, A Handbook of. By CATHERINE J. WOOD. *Cheap Edition.* 1s. 6d.; cloth, 2s.
Nursing of Sick Children, A Handbook for the. By CATHERINE J. WOOD. 2s. 6d.
Oil Painting, A Manual of. By the Hon. JOHN COLLIER. 2s. 6d.
Our Own Country. Six Vols. With 1,200 Illustrations. 7s. 6d. each.
Pactolus Prime. A Novel. By ALBION W. TOURGÉE. 5s.
Painting, The English School of. By ERNEST CHESNEAU. 5s.
Painting, Practical Guides to. With Coloured Plates:—

MARINE PAINTING. 5s.
ANIMAL PAINTING. 5s.
CHINA PAINTING. 5s.
FIGURE PAINTING. 7s. 6d.
ELEMENTARY FLOWER PAINTING. 3s.
FLOWER PAINTING, Two Books, 5s. each.
TREE PAINTING. 5s.
WATER-COLOUR PAINTING. 5s.
NEUTRAL TINT. 5s.
SEPIA, in Two Vols., 3s. each; or in One Vol., 5s.
FLOWERS, AND HOW TO PAINT THEM. 5s.

Paxton's Flower Garden. By Sir JOSEPH PAXTON and Prof. LINDLEY. With 100 Coloured Plates. *Price on application.*
People I've Smiled with. By MARSHALL P. WILDER. 2s.; cloth, 2s. 6d.
Peoples of the World, The. In Six Vols. By Dr. ROBERT BROWN. Illustrated. 7s. 6d. each.
Phantom City, The. By W. WESTALL. 5s.
Phillips, Watts, Artist and Playwright. By Miss E. WATTS PHILLIPS. With 32 Plates. 10s. 6d.
Photography for Amateurs. By T. C. HEPWORTH. Illustrated. 1s.; or cloth, 1s. 6d.
Phrase and Fable, Dictionary of. By the Rev. Dr. BREWER. *Cheap Edition, Enlarged,* cloth, 3s. 6d.; or with leather back, 4s. 6d.
Picturesque America. Complete in Four Vols., with 48 Exquisite Steel Plates and about 800 Original Wood Engravings. £2 2s. each.
Picturesque Australasia, Cassell's. With upwards of 1,000 Illustrations. Complete in Four Vols. 7s. 6d. each.
Picturesque Canada. With 600 Original Illustrations. 2 Vols. £3 3s. each.
Picturesque Europe. Complete in Five Vols. Each containing 13 Exquisite Steel Plates, from Original Drawings, and nearly 200 Original Illustrations. ORIGINAL EDITION. Cloth, £21; half-morocco, £31 10s.; morocco gilt, £52 10s. The POPULAR EDITION is published in Five Vols., 18s. each.
Picturesque Mediterranean. With Magnificent Original Illustrations by the leading Artists of the Day. Complete in Two Vols. £2 2s. each.
Pigeon Keeper, The Practical. By LEWIS WRIGHT. Illustrated. 3s. 6d.

Selections from Cassell & Company's Publications.

Pigeons, The Book of. By ROBERT FULTON. Edited and Arranged by L. WRIGHT. With 50 Coloured Plates, 31s. 6d.; half-morocco, £2 2s.
Poems, Aubrey de Vere's. A Selection. Edited by J. DENNIS. 3s. 6d.
Poets, Cassell's Miniature Library of the:—
   BURNS. Two Vols. 2s. 6d. | MILTON. Two Vols. 2s. 6d.
   BYRON. Two Vols. 2s. 6d. | SCOTT. Two Vols. 2s. 6d. [2s. 6d.
   HOOD. Two Vols. 2s. 6d. | SHERIDAN and GOLDSMITH. 2 Vols.
   LONGFELLOW. Two Vols. 2s. 6d. | WORDSWORTH. Two Vols. 2s. 6d.
   SHAKESPEARE, Illustrated. In 12 Vols., in Case, 12s.
Police Code, and Manual of the Criminal Law. By C. E. HOWARD VINCENT, M.P. 2s.
Polytechnic Series, The.
   Forty Lessons in Carpentry Workshop Practice. Cloth gilt, 1s.
   Practical Plane and Solid Geometry, including Graphic Arithmetic. Vol. I., Elementary Stage. Cloth gilt, 3s.
   Forty Lessons in Engineering Workshop Practice, 1s. 6d.
   Technical Scales. Set of Ten in cloth case, 1s. Also on Celluloid in Case, 10s. 6d. the set.
   Elementary Chemistry for Science Schools and Classes. Crown 8vo, 1s. 6d.
   Building Construction Plates. A Series of 40 Drawings. Royal folio size, 1½d. each.
Portrait Gallery, The Cabinet. First and Second Series, each containing 36 Cabinet Photographs of Eminent Men and Women. With Biographical Sketches. 15s. each.
Poultry Keeper, The Practical. By L. WRIGHT. Illustrated. 3s. 6d.
Poultry, The Book of. By LEWIS WRIGHT. *Popular Edition.* 10s. 6d.
Poultry, The Illustrated Book of. By LEWIS WRIGHT. With Fifty Coloured Plates. *New and Revised Edition.* Cloth, 31s. 6d.
Queen Summer; or, The Tourney of the Lily and the Rose. Penned and Portrayed by WALTER CRANE. With Forty Pages of Designs in Colours. 6s. *Large Paper Edition*, 21s. net.
Queen Victoria, The Life and Times of. By ROBERT WILSON. Complete in Two Vols. With numerous Illustrations. 9s. each.
Rabbit-Keeper, The Practical. By CUNICULUS. Illustrated. 3s. 6d.
Railway Guides, Official Illustrated. With Illustrations, Maps, &c. Price 1s. each; or in cloth, 2s. each.
   GREAT WESTERN RAILWAY. | LONDON AND SOUTH-WESTERN RAILWAY.
   GREAT NORTHERN RAILWAY.
   LONDON, BRIGHTON AND SOUTH COAST RAILWAY. | MIDLAND RAILWAY.
   LONDON AND NORTH-WESTERN RAILWAY. | SOUTH-EASTERN RAILWAY.
      | GREAT EASTERN RAILWAY.
Railway Library, Cassell's. Crown 8vo, boards, 2s. each.
   THE ASTONISHING HISTORY OF TROY TOWN. By Q. | JACK GORDON, KNIGHT ERRANT, GOTHAM, 1883. By BARCLAY NORTH.
   THE ADMIRABLE LADY BIDDY FANE. By FRANK BARRETT. | THE DIAMOND BUTTON. By BARCLAY NORTH.
   COMMODORE JUNK. By G. MANVILLE FENN. | ANOTHER'S CRIME. By JULIAN H. W. THORNE.
   ST. CUTHBERT'S TOWER. By FLORENCE WARDEN. | THE YOKE OF THE THORAH. By SIDNEY LUSKA.
   THE MAN WITH A THUMB. By BARCLAY NORTH. | WHO IS JOHN NOMAN? By CHARLES HENRY BECKETT.
   BY RIGHT NOT LAW. By R. SHERARD. | THE TRAGEDY OF BRINKWATER. By MARTHA L. MOODEY.
   WITHIN SOUND OF THE WEIR. By THOMAS ST. E. HAKE. | AN AMERICAN PENMAN. By JULIAN HAWTHORNE.
   UNDER A STRANGE MASK. By FRANK BARRETT. | SECTION 558; or, THE FATAL LETTER. By JULIAN HAWTHORNE.
   THE COOMBSBERROW MYSTERY. By JAMES COLWALL. | THE BROWN STONE BOY. By W. H. BISHOP.
   DEAD MAN'S ROCK. By Q.
   A QUEER RACE. By W. WESTALL. | A TRAGIC MYSTERY. By JULIAN HAWTHORNE.
   CAPTAIN TRAFALGAR. By WESTALL and LAURIE.
   THE PHANTOM CITY. By W. WESTALL. | THE GREAT BANK ROBBERY. By JULIAN HAWTHORNE.
Redgrave, Richard, C.B., R.A. Memoir. Compiled from his Diary. By F. M. REDGRAVE. 10s. 6d.

Selections from Cassell & Company's Publications.

Richard, Henry, M.P. A Biography. By CHARLES S. MIALL. 7s. 6d.
Rivers of Great Britain: Descriptive, Historical, Pictorial. RIVERS OF THE EAST COAST. 42s.
Rivers of Great Britain: The Royal River: The Thames, from Source to Sea. With Descriptive Text and a Series of beautiful Engravings. *Original Edition*, £2 2s.; *Popular Edition*, 16s.
Robinson Crusoe, Cassell's New Fine-Art Edition of. With upwards of 100 Original Illustrations. 7s. 6d.
Rossetti, Dante Gabriel, as Designer and Writer. Notes by WILLIAM MICHAEL ROSSETTI. 7s. 6d.
Russia, Through, on a Mustang. By THOMAS STEVENS. 7s. 6d.
Russo-Turkish War, Cassell's History of. With about 500 Illustrations. Two Vols. 9s. each.
Saturday Journal, Cassell's. Yearly Volume, cloth, 7s. 6d.
Science for All. Edited by Dr. ROBERT BROWN. *Revised Edition.* Illustrated. Five Vols. 9s. each.
Sculpture, A Primer of. By E. ROSCOE MULLINS. With Illustrations, 2s. 6d.
Sea, The: Its Stirring Story of Adventure, Peril, and Heroism. By F. WHYMPER. With 400 Illustrations. Four Vols. 7s. 6d. each.
Secret of the Lamas, The. A Tale of Thibet. Crown 8vo, 5s.
Shaftesbury, The Seventh Earl of, K.G., The Life and Work of. By EDWIN HODDER. Three Vols., 36s. *Popular Edition*, One Vol., 7s. 6d.
Shakespeare, The Plays of. Edited by Professor HENRY MORLEY. Complete in 13 Vols., cloth, 21s.; half-morocco, cloth sides, 42s.
Shakespeare, Cassell's Quarto Edition. Containing about 600 Illustrations by H. C. SELOUS. Complete in Three Vols., cloth gilt, £3 3s.
Shakespeare, Miniature. Illustrated. In Twelve Vols., in box, 12s.; or in Red Paste Grain (box to match), with spring catch, 21s.
Shakespeare, The England of. By E. GOADBY. Illustrated. 2s. 6d.
Shakspere, The International. *Edition de Luxe.*
"OTHELLO." Illustrated by FRANK DICKSEE, R.A. £3 10s.
"KING HENRY IV." Illustrated by EDUARD GRÜTZNER, £3 10s.
"AS YOU LIKE IT." Illustrated by ÉMILE BAYARD, £3 10s.
"ROMEO AND JULIET." Illustrated by F. DICKSEE, R.A. Is now out of print, and scarce.
Shakspere, The Leopold. With 400 Illustrations. *Cheap Edition.* 3s. 6d. Cloth gilt, gilt edges, 5s.; Roxburgh, 7s. 6d.
Shakspere, The Royal. With Steel Plates and Wood Engravings. Three Vols. 15s. each.
Social Welfare, Subjects of. By Sir LYON PLAYFAIR, K.C.B. 7s. 6d.
Splendid Spur, The. Edited by Q. Illustrated. 3s. 6d.
Standard Library, Cassell's. Stiff covers, 1s. each; cloth, 2s. each.

Coningsby.	Adventures of Mr. Ledbury.	Eugene Aram.
Mary Barton.	Ivanhoe.	Jack Hinton.
The Antiquary.	Oliver Twist.	Poe's Works.
Nicholas Nickleby (Two Vols.).	Selections from Hood's Works.	Old Mortality.
Jane Eyre.	Longfellow's Prose Works.	The Hour and the Man.
Wuthering Heights.	Sense and Sensibility.	Handy Andy.
Dombey and Son (Two Vols.)	Lytton's Plays.	Scarlet Letter.
The Prairie.	Tales, Poems, and Sketches. Bret Harte.	Pickwick (Two Vols.).
Night and Morning.	Martin Chuzzlewit (Two Vols.).	Last of the Mohicans.
Kenilworth.	The Prince of the House of David.	Pride and Prejudice.
Ingoldsby Legends.	Sheridan's Plays.	Yellowplush Papers.
Tower of London.	Uncle Tom's Cabin.	Tales of the Borders.
The Pioneers.	Deerslayer.	Last Days of Palmyra.
Charles O'Malley.	Rome and the Early Christians.	Washington Irving's Sketch-Book.
Barnaby Rudge.	The Trials of Margaret Lyndsay.	The Talisman.
Cakes and Ale.	Harry Lorrequer.	Rienzi.
The King's Own.		Old Curiosity Shop.
People I have Met.		Heart of Midlothian.
The Pathfinder.		Last Days of Pompeii.
Evelina.		American Humour.
Scott's Poems.		Sketches by Boz.
Last of the Barons.		Macaulay's Lays and Essays.

Selections from Cassell & Company's Publications.

Sports and Pastimes, Cassell's Complete Book of. *Cheap Edition.* With more than 900 Illustrations. Medium 8vo, 992 pages, cloth, 3s. 6d.
Stanley in East Africa, Scouting for. By T. STEVENS. With 14 Illustrations. Cloth, 7s. 6d.
Star-Land. By Sir ROBERT STAWELL BALL, LL.D., F.R.S., F.R.A.S. Illustrated. Crown 8vo, 6s.
Steam Engine, The. By W. H. NORTHCOTT, C.E. 3s. 6d.
Storehouse of General Information, Cassell's. With Wood Engravings, Maps, and Coloured Plates. In Vols., 5s. each.
Story of Francis Cludde, The. A Novel. By STANLEY J. WEYMAN. 7s. 6d. net.
Story Poems. For Young and Old. Edited by Miss E. DAVENPORT ADAMS. 6s.
Strange Doings in Strange Places. Complete Sensational Stories. 5s.
Teaching in Three Continents. Personal Notes on the Educational Systems of the World. By W. C. GRASBY. 6s.
Technical Education. By F. C. MONTAGUE. 6d.
Thackeray, Character Sketches from. Six New and Original Drawings by FREDERICK BARNARD, reproduced in Photogravure. 21s.
The "Short Story" Library.

Noughts and Crosses. By Q. 5s.	Eleven Possible Cases. By Various Authors. 6s.
Otto the Knight, &c. By OCTAVE THANET. 5s.	Felicia. By Miss FANNY MURFREE. 5s.
Fourteen to One, &c. By ELIZABETH STUART PHELPS. 5s.	The Poet's Audience, and Delilah. By CLARA SAVILE CLARKE. 5s.

Treasure Island. By R. L. STEVENSON. Illustrated, 3s. 6d.
Trees, Familiar. By G. S. BOULGER, F.L.S. Two Series. With 40 full-page Coloured Plates by W. H. J. BOOT. 12s. 6d. each.
"Unicode": the Universal Telegraphic Phrase Book. *Desk or Pocket Edition.* 2s. 6d.
United States, Cassell's History of the. By the late EDMUND OLLIER. With 600 Illustrations. Three Vols. 9s. each.
Universal History, Cassell's Illustrated. Four Vols. 9s. each.
Vicar of Wakefield and other Works by OLIVER GOLDSMITH. Illustrated. 3s. 6d.; cloth, gilt edges, 5s.
Vision of Saints, A. *Edition de Luxe.* By LEWIS MORRIS. With 20 Full-Page Illustrations. 21s.
Waterloo Letters. Edited by MAJOR-GENERAL H. T. SIBORNE, late Colonel R.E. With numerous Plans of the Battlefield. 21s.
Web of Gold, A. By KATHARINE PEARSON WOODS. Crown 8vo, 6s.
What Girls Can Do. By PHYLLIS BROWNE. 2s. 6d.
Wild Birds, Familiar. By W. SWAYSLAND. Four Series. With 40 Coloured Plates in each. 12s. 6d. each.
Wild Flowers, Familiar. By F. E. HULME, F.L.S., F.S.A. Five Series. With 40 Coloured Plates in each. 12s. 6d. each.
Wood, Rev. J. G., Life of the. By the Rev. THEODORE WOOD. Extra crown 8vo, cloth. *Cheap Edition.* 5s.
Work. An Illustrated Magazine for all Workmen. Yearly Vol., 7s. 6d.
World of Wit and Humour, The. With 400 Illustrations. 7s. 6d.
World of Wonders. Two Vols. With 400 Illustrations. 7s. 6d. each.
Yule Tide. Cassell's Christmas Annual. 1s.

ILLUSTRATED MAGAZINES.

The Quiver. ENLARGED SERIES. Monthly, 6d.
Cassell's Family Magazine. Monthly, 7d.
"Little Folks" Magazine. Monthly, 6d.
The Magazine of Art. Monthly, 1s.
Cassell's Saturday Journal. Weekly, 1d.; Monthly, 6d.
Work. Weekly, 1d.; Monthly, 6d.

CASSELL'S COMPLETE CATALOGUE, containing particulars of upwards of One Thousand Volumes, will be sent post free on application.

CASSELL & COMPANY, LIMITED, *Ludgate Hill, London.*

Selections from Cassell & Company's Publications.

Bibles and Religious Works.

Bible, Cassell's Illustrated Family. With 900 Illustrations. Leather, gilt edges, £2 10s.
Bible Dictionary, Cassell's. With nearly 600 Illustrations. 7s. 6d.
Bible Educator, The. Edited by the Very Rev. Dean PLUMPTRE, D.D., Wells. With Illustrations, Maps, &c. Four Vols., cloth, 6s. each.
Bible Student in the British Museum, The. By the Rev. J. G. KITCHIN, M.A. 1s.
Biblewomen and Nurses. Yearly Volume. Illustrated. 3s.
Bunyan's Pilgrim's Progress and Holy War. With 200 Illustrations. With a New Life of Bunyan by the Rev. JOHN BROWN, B.A., D.D. Cloth, 16s.
Bunyan's Pilgrim's Progress (Cassell's Illustrated). 4to, 7s. 6d.
Bunyan's Pilgrim's Progress. With Illustrations. Cloth, 2s. 6d.
Child's Bible, The. With 200 Illustrations. 150*th Thousand.* 7s. 6d.
Child's Life of Christ, The. With 200 Illustrations. 7s. 6d.
"Come, ye Children." Illustrated. By Rev. BENJAMIN WAUGH. 5s.
Conquests of the Cross. With numerous Illustrations. Complete in Three Vols. 9s. each.
Doré Bible. With 238 Illustrations by GUSTAVE DORÉ. Small folio, best morocco, gilt edges, £15.
Early Days of Christianity, The. By the Ven. Archdeacon FARRAR, D.D., F.R.S. LIBRARY EDITION. Two Vols., 24s.; morocco, £2 2s. POPULAR EDITION. Complete in One Volume, cloth, 6s.; cloth, gilt edges, 7s. 6d.; Persian morocco, 10s. 6d.; tree-calf, 15s.
Family Prayer-Book, The. Edited by Rev. Canon GARBETT, M.A., and Rev. S. MARTIN. Extra crown 4to, cloth, 5s.; morocco, 18s.
Gleanings after Harvest. Studies and Sketches by the Rev. JOHN R. VERNON, M.A. 6s.
"Graven in the Rock." By the Rev. Dr. SAMUEL KINNS, F.R.A.S., Author of "Moses and Geology." Illustrated. 12s. 6d.
"Heart Chords." A Series of Works by Eminent Divines. Bound in cloth, red edges, One Shilling each.

MY BIBLE. By the Right Rev. W. BOYD CARPENTER, Bishop of Ripon.
MY FATHER. By the Right Rev. ASHTON OXENDEN, late Bishop of Montreal.
MY WORK FOR GOD. By the Right Rev. Bishop COTTERILL.
MY OBJECT IN LIFE. By the Ven. Archdeacon FARRAR, D.D.
MY ASPIRATIONS. By the Rev. G. MATHESON, D.D.
MY EMOTIONAL LIFE. By the Rev. Preb. CHADWICK, D.D.
MY BODY. By the Rev. Prof. W. G. BLAIKIE, D.D.
MY GROWTH IN DIVINE LIFE. By the Rev. Preb. REYNOLDS, M.A.
MY SOUL. By the Rev. P. B. POWER, M.A.
MY HEREAFTER. By the Very Rev. Dean BICKERSTETH.
MY WALK WITH GOD. By the Very Rev. Dean MONTGOMERY.
MY AIDS TO THE DIVINE LIFE. By the Very Rev. Dean BOYLE.
MY SOURCES OF STRENGTH. By the Rev. E. E. JENKINS, M.A., Secretary of Wesleyan Missionary Society.

Helps to Belief. A Series of Helpful Manuals on the Religious Difficulties of the Day. Edited by the Rev. TEIGNMOUTH SHORE, M.A., Canon of Worcester, and Chaplain-in-Ordinary to the Queen. Cloth, 1s. each.

CREATION. By the Lord Bishop of Carlisle.
THE DIVINITY OF OUR LORD. By the Lord Bishop of Derry.
THE MORALITY OF THE OLD TESTAMENT. By the Rev. Newman Smyth, D.D.
MIRACLES. By the Rev. Brownlow Maitland, M.A.
PRAYER. By the Rev. T. Teignmouth Shore, M.A.
THE ATONEMENT. By William Connor Magee, D.D., Late Archbishop of York.

Selections from Cassell & Company's Publications.

Holy Land and the Bible, The. By the Rev. CUNNINGHAM GEIKIE, D.D. Two Vols., with Map, 24s. *Illustrated Edition*, One Vol., 21s.

Lectures on Christianity and Socialism. By the Right Rev. ALFRED BARRY, D.D. Cloth, 3s. 6d.

Life of Christ, The. By the Ven. Archdeacon FARRAR, D.D., F.R.S. ILLUSTRATED EDITION, morocco antique, 42s. CHEAP ILLUSTRATED EDITION. Cloth, 7s. 6d.; cloth, full gilt, gilt edges, 10s. 6d. LIBRARY EDITION. Two Vols. Cloth, 24s.; morocco, 42s. POPULAR EDITION, in One Vol., 8vo, cloth, 6s.; cloth, gilt edges, 7s. 6d.; Persian morocco, gilt edges, 10s. 6d.; tree-calf, 15s.

Marriage Ring, The. By WILLIAM LANDELS, D.D. *New and Cheaper Edition.* 3s. 6d.

Moses and Geology; or, The Harmony of the Bible with Science. By the Rev. SAMUEL KINNS, Ph.D., F.R.A.S. Illustrated. *Cheap Edition*, 6s.

My Comfort in Sorrow. By HUGH MACMILLAN, D.D., LL.D., F.R.S.E., &c. Cloth, 1s.

New Testament Commentary for English Readers, The. Edited by the Rt. Rev. C. J. ELLICOTT, D.D., Lord Bishop of Gloucester and Bristol. In Three Volumes. 21s. each. Vol. I.—The Four Gospels. Vol. II.—The Acts, Romans, Corinthians, Galatians. Vol. III.—The remaining Books of the New Testament.

New Testament Commentary. Edited by Bishop ELLICOTT. Handy Volume Edition. St. Matthew, 3s. 6d. St. Mark, 3s. St. Luke, 3s. 6d. St. John, 3s. 6d. The Acts of the Apostles, 3s. 6d. Romans, 2s. 6d. Corinthians I. and II., 3s. Galatians, Ephesians, and Philippians, 3s. Colossians, Thessalonians, and Timothy, 3s. Titus, Philemon, Hebrews, and James, 3s. Peter, Jude, and John, 3s. The Revelation, 3s. An Introduction to the New Testament, 3s. 6d.

Old Testament Commentary for English Readers, The. Edited by the Right Rev. C. J. ELLICOTT, D.D., Lord Bishop of Gloucester and Bristol. Complete in Five Vols. 21s. each. Vol. I.—Genesis to Numbers. Vol. II.—Deuteronomy to Samuel II. Vol. III.—Kings I. to Esther. Vol. IV.—Job to Isaiah. Vol. V.—Jeremiah to Malachi.

Old Testament Commentary. Edited by Bishop ELLICOTT. Handy Volume Edition. Genesis, 3s. 6d. Exodus, 3s. Leviticus, 3s. Numbers, 2s. 6d. Deuteronomy, 2s. 6d.

Protestantism, The History of. By the Rev. J. A. WYLIE, LL.D. Containing upwards of 600 Original Illustrations. Three Vols. 9s. each.

Quiver Yearly Volume, The. 250 high-class Illustrations. 7s. 6d.

Religion, The Dictionary of. By the Rev. W. BENHAM, B.D. *Cheap Edition.* 10s. 6d.

St. George for England; and other Sermons preached to Children. By the Rev. T. TEIGNMOUTH SHORE, M.A., Canon of Worcester. 5s.

St. Paul, The Life and Work of. By the Ven. Archdeacon FARRAR, D.D., F.R.S., Chaplain-in-Ordinary to the Queen. LIBRARY EDITION. Two Vols., cloth, 24s.; calf, 42s. ILLUSTRATED EDITION, complete in One Volume, with about 300 Illustrations, £1 1s.; morocco, £2 2s. POPULAR EDITION. One Volume, 8vo, cloth, 6s.; cloth, gilt edges, 7s. 6d.; Persian morocco, 10s. 6d.; tree-calf, 15s.

Shall We Know One Another in Heaven? By the Rt. Rev. J. C. RYLE, D.D., Bishop of Liverpool. *Cheap Edition.* Paper covers, 6d.

Signa Christi: Evidences of Christianity set forth in the Person and Work of Christ. By the Rev. JAMES AITCHISON. 5s.

"Sunday," Its Origin, History, and Present Obligation. By the Ven. Archdeacon HESSEY, D.C.L. *Fifth Edition.* 7s. 6d.

Twilight of Life, The. Words of Counsel and Comfort for the Aged. By the Rev. JOHN ELLERTON, M.A. 1s. 6d.

Selections from Cassell & Company's Publications.

Educational Works and Students' Manuals.

Agricultural Series, Cassell's. Edited by JOHN WRIGHTSON, Professor of Agriculture.
   Crops. By Professor WRIGHTSON. 2s. 6d.
   Soils and Manures. By J. M. H. MUNRO, D.Sc. (London), F.I.C., F.C.S. 2s. 6d.
Alphabet, Cassell's Pictorial. 3s. 6d.
Arithmetics, The Modern School. By GEORGE RICKS, B.Sc. Lond. With Test Cards. (*List on application.*)
Atlas, Cassell's Popular. Containing 24 Coloured Maps. 3s. 6d.
Book-Keeping. By THEODORE JONES. For Schools, 2s.; cloth, 3s. For the Million, 2s.; cloth, 3s. Books for Jones's System, 2s.
Chemistry, The Public School. By J. H. ANDERSON, M.A. 2s. 6d.
Classical Texts for Schools, Cassell's. (*A List post free on application.*)
Cookery for Schools. By LIZZIE HERITAGE. 6d.
Copy-Books, Cassell's Graduated. *Eighteen Books.* 2d. each.
Copy-Books, The Modern School. *Twelve Books.* 2d. each.
Drawing Copies, Cassell's Modern School Freehand. First Grade, 1s.; Second Grade, 2s.
Drawing Copies, Cassell's "New Standard." *Complete in Fourteen Books.* 2d., 3d., and 4d. each.
Electricity, Practical. By Prof. W. E. AYRTON. 7s. 6d.
Energy and Motion. By WILLIAM PAICE, M.A. Illustrated. 1s. 6d.
English Literature, First Sketch of. By Prof. MORLEY. 7s. 6d.
English Literature, The Story of. By ANNA BUCKLAND. 3s. 6d.
Euclid, Cassell's. Edited by Prof. WALLACE, M.A. 1s.
Euclid, The First Four Books of. *New Edition.* In paper, 6d.; cloth, 9d.
Experimental Geometry. By PAUL BERT. Illustrated. 1s. 6d.
French, Cassell's Lessons in. *New and Revised Edition.* Parts I. and II., each 2s. 6d.; complete, 4s. 6d. Key, 1s. 6d.
French-English and English-French Dictionary. *Entirely New and Enlarged Edition.* 1,150 pages, 8vo, cloth, 3s. 6d.
French Reader, Cassell's Public School. By G. S. CONRAD. 2s. 6d.
Gaudeamus. Songs for Colleges and Schools. Edited by JOHN FARMER. 5s. Words only, paper covers, 6d.; cloth, 9d.
German Dictionary, Cassell's New. German-English, English-German. *Cheap Edition.* Cloth, 3s. 6d.
German of To-Day. By Dr. HEINEMANN. 1s. 6d.
German Reading, First Lessons in. By A. JAGST. Illustrated. 1s.
Hand-and-Eye Training. By G. RICKS, B.Sc. 2 Vols., with 16 Coloured Plates in each Vol. Cr. 4to, 6s. each. Cards for Class Use, 5 sets, 1s. each.
"Hand-and-Eye Training Cards." Five Sets in Case. 1s. each.
Handbook of New Code of Regulations. By J. F. MOSS. 1s.; cloth, 2s.
Historical Cartoons, Cassell's Coloured. Size 45 in. × 35 in., 2s. each. Mounted on canvas and varnished, with rollers, 5s. each.
Historical Course for Schools, Cassell's. Illustrated throughout. I.—Stories from English History, 1s. II.—The Simple Outline of English History, 1s. 3d. III.—The Class History of England, 2s. 6d.
Latin-English Dictionary, Cassell's. By J. R. V. MARCHANT, 3s. 6d.
Latin Primer, The First. By Prof. POSTGATE. 1s.
Latin Primer, The New. By Prof. J. P. POSTGATE. Crown 8vo, 2s. 6d.
Latin Prose for Lower Forms. By M. A. BAYFIELD, M.A. 2s. 6d.
Laundry Work (How to Teach It). By Mrs. E. LORD. 6d.
Laws of Every-Day Life. By H. O. ARNOLD-FORSTER. 1s. 6d.
Little Folks' History of England. Illustrated. 1s. 6d.
Making of the Home, The. By Mrs. SAMUEL A. BARNETT. 1s. 6d.
Map-Building Series, Cassell's. Outline Maps prepared by H. O. ARNOLD-FORSTER. Per Set of Twelve, 1s.

Selections from Cassell & Company's Publications.

Marlborough Books:—Arithmetic Examples, 3s. Arithmetic Rules, 1s. 6d. French Exercises, 3s. 6d. French Grammar, 2s. 6d. German do., 3s. 6d.

Mechanics for Young Beginners, A First Book of. By the Rev. J. G. Easton, M.A. 4s. 6d.

Mechanics and Machine Design, Numerical Examples in Practical. By R. G. Blaine, M.E. With Diagrams. Cloth, 2s. 6d.

"Model Joint" Wall Sheets, for Instruction in Manual Training. By S. Barter. Eight Sheets, 2s. 6d. each.

Natural History Coloured Wall Sheets, Cassell's New. 18 Subjects. Size, 39 by 31 in. Mounted on rollers and varnished. 3s. each.

Object Lessons from Nature. By Prof. L. C. Miall, F.L.S. 2s. 6d.

Physiology for Schools. By Alfred T. Schofield, M.D., M.R.C.S. 1s. 9d.; Three Parts, paper covers, 5d. each.

Poetry Readers, Cassell's New. Illustrated. 12 Books. 1d. each.

Popular Educator, Cassell's NEW. With Revised Text, New Maps, New Coloured Plates, New Type, &c. To be completed in 8 Vols. 5s. each.

Readers, Cassell's "Higher Class." (*List on application.*)

Readers, Cassell's Historical. Illustrated. (*List on application.*)

Readers, Cassell's Readable. Illustrated. (*List on application.*)

Readers for Infant Schools, Coloured. Three Books. 4d. each.

Reader, The Citizen. By H. O. Arnold-Forster. Illustrated. 1s. 6d.

Reader, The Empire. By G. R. Parkin. 1s. 6d.

Reader, The Temperance. By Rev. J. Dennis Hird. Cr. 8vo, 1s. 6d.

Readers, The "Modern School" Geographical. (*List on application.*)

Readers, The "Modern School." Illustrated. (*List on application.*)

Reckoning, Howard's Anglo-American Art of. By C. Frusher Howard. Paper covers, 1s.; cloth, 2s. *Large Paper Edition*, 5s.

Round World, The. By H. O. Arnold-Forster. 3s. 6d.

School Certificates, Cassell's. Three Colours, $6\frac{1}{4} \times 4\frac{3}{4}$ in., 1d.; Five Colours, $11\frac{3}{4} \times 9\frac{1}{4}$ in., 3d.; Seven Colours and Gold, $9\frac{3}{4} \times 6\frac{1}{4}$ in., 3d.

Science Applied to Work. By J. A. Bower. 1s.

Science of Everyday Life. By J. A. Bower. Illustrated. 1s.

Shade from Models, Common Objects, and Casts of Ornament, How to. By W. E. Sparkes. With 25 Plates by the Author. 3s.

Shakspere's Plays for School Use. 5 Books. Illustrated. 6d. each.

Shakspere Reading Book, The. Illustrated. 3s. 6d.

Spelling, A Complete Manual of. By J. D. Morell, LL.D. 1s.

Technical Manuals, Cassell's. Illustrated throughout:—
Handrailing and Staircasing, 3s. 6d.—Bricklayers, Drawing for, 3s.—Building Construction, 2s.—Cabinet-Makers, Drawing for, 3s.—Carpenters and Joiners, Drawing for, 3s. 6d.—Gothic Stonework, 3s.—Linear Drawing and Practical Geometry, 2s.—Linear Drawing and Projection. The Two Vols. in One, 3s. 6d.—Machinists and Engineers, Drawing for, 4s. 6d.—Metal Plate Workers, Drawing for, 3s.—Model Drawing, 3s.—Orthographical and Isometrical Projection, 2s.—Practical Perspective, 3s.—Stonemasons, Drawing for, 3s.—Applied Mechanics, by Sir R. S. Ball, LL.D., 2s.—Systematic Drawing and Shading, 2s.

Technical Educator, Cassell's. *Revised Edition.* Four Vols. 5s. each.

Technology, Manuals of. Edited by Prof. Ayrton, F.R.S., and Richard Wormell, D.Sc., M.A. Illustrated throughout:—
The Dyeing of Textile Fabrics, by Prof. Hummel, 5s.—Watch and Clock Making, by D. Glasgow, Vice-President of the British Horological Institute, 4s. 6d.—Steel and Iron, by Prof. W. H. Greenwood, F.C.S., M.I.C.E., &c., 5s.—Spinning Woollen and Worsted, by W. S. B. McLaren, M.P., 4s. 6d.—Design in Textile Fabrics, by T. R. Ashenhurst, 4s. 6d.—Practical Mechanics, by Prof. Perry, M.E., 3s. 6d.—Cutting Tools Worked by Hand and Machine, by Prof. Smith, 3s. 6d. (*A Prospectus on application.*)

CASSELL & COMPANY, Limited, *Ludgate Hill, London.*

Selections from Cassell & Company's Publications.

Books for Young People.

"**Little Folks**" **Half-Yearly Volume.** Containing 432 4to pages, with about 200 Illustrations, and Pictures in Colour. Boards, 3s. 6d.; cloth, 5s.

Bo-Peep. A Book for the Littl Ones. With Original Stories and Verses. Illustrated throughout. Yearly Volume. Boards, 2s. 6d.; cloth, 3s. 6d.

Pleasant Work for Busy Fingers. By MAGGIE BROWNE. Illustrated. 5s.

Cassell's Pictorial Scrap Book, containing several thousand Pictures. Coloured boards, 15s.; cloth lettered, 21s. Also in Six Sectional Vols., 3s. 6d. each.

The Marvellous Budget: being 65,536 Stories of Jack and Jill. By the Rev. F. BENNETT. Illustrated. 2s. 6d.

Schoolroom and Home Theatricals. By ARTHUR WAUGH. Illustrated. 2s. 6d.

Magic at Home. By Prof. HOFFMAN. Illustrated. Cloth gilt, 5s.

"**Little Folks**" **Painting Book, The New.** Containing nearly 350 Outline Illustrations suitable for Colouring. 1s.

Little Mother Bunch. By Mrs. MOLESWORTH. Illustrated. Cloth, 3s. 6d.

Ships, Sailors, and the Sea. By R. J. CORNEWALL-JONES. *Cheap Edition.* Illustrated. Cloth, 2s. 6d.

Famous Sailors of Former Times. By CLEMENTS MARKHAM. Illustrated. 2s. 6d.

The Tales of the Sixty Mandarins. By P. V. RAMASWAMI RAJU. With an Introduction by Prof. HENRY MORLEY. Illustrated. 5s.

Pictures of School Life and Boyhood. Selected from the best Authors. Edited by PERCY FITZGERALD, M.A. 2s. 6d.

Heroes of Every-day Life. By LAURA LANE. With about 20 Full-page Illustrations. Cloth. 2s. 6d.

Books for Young People. Illustrated. Cloth gilt, 5s. each.

- The Champion of Odin; or, Viking Life in the Days of Old. By J. Fred. Hodgetts.
- The Romance of Invention. By James Burnley.
- Under Bayard's Banner. By Henry Frith.
- Bound by a Spell; or, The Hunted Witch of the Forest. By the Hon. Mrs. Greene.

Books for Young People. Illustrated. 3s. 6d. each.

- The White House at Inch Gow. By Mrs. Pitt.
- A Sweet Girl Graduate. By L. T. Meade.
- The King's Command: A Story for Girls. By Maggie Symington.
- Lost in Samoa. A Tale of Adventure in the Navigator Islands. By Edward S. Ellis.
- Tad; or, "Getting Even" with Him. By Edward S. Ellis.
- For Fortune and Glory: A Story of the Soudan War. By Lewis Hough.
- Polly: A New-Fashioned Girl. By L. T. Meade.
- "Follow My Leader." By Talbot Baines Reed.
- The Cost of a Mistake. By Sarah Pitt.
- A World of Girls: The Story of a School. By L. T. Meade.
- Lost among White Africans. By David Ker.
- The Palace Beautiful. By L. T. Meade.
- On Board the "Esmeralda." By John C. Hutcheson.
- In Quest of Gold. By A. St. Johnston.

Crown 8vo Library. *Cheap Editions.* 2s. 6d. each.

- Rambles Round London. By C. L. Matéaux. Illustrated.
- Around and About Old England. By C. L. Matéaux. Illustrated.
- Paws and Claws. By one of the Authors of "Poems written for a Child." Illustrated.
- Decisive Events in History. By Thomas Archer. With Original Illustrations.
- The True Robinson Crusoes. Cloth gilt.
- Peeps Abroad for Folks at Home. Illustrated throughout.
- Wild Adventures in Wild Places. By Dr. Gordon Stables, R.N. Illustrated.
- Modern Explorers. By Thomas Frost. Illustrated. *New and Cheaper Edition.*
- Early Explorers. By Thomas Frost.
- Home Chat with our Young Folks. Illustrated throughout.
- Jungle, Peak, and Plain. Illustrated throughout.
- The England of Shakespeare. By E. Goadby. With Full-page Illustrations.

Selections from Cassell & Company's Publications.

The "Cross and Crown" Series. Illustrated. 2s. 6d. each.

Freedom's Sword: A Story of the Days of Wallace and Bruce. By Annie S. Swan.
Strong to Suffer: A Story of the Jews. By E. Wynne.
Heroes of the Indian Empire; or, Stories of Valour and Victory. By Ernest Foster.
In Letters of Flame: A Story of the Waldenses. By C. L. Matéaux.
Through Trial to Triumph. By Madeline B. Hunt.
By Fire and Sword: A Story of the Huguenots. By Thomas Archer.
Adam Hepburn's Vow: A Tale of Kirk and Covenant. By Annie S. Swan.
No. XIII.; or, The Story of the Lost Vestal. A Tale of Early Christian Days. By Emma Marshall.

"Golden Mottoes" Series, The. Each Book containing 208 pages, with Four full-page Original Illustrations. Crown 8vo, cloth gilt, 2s. each.

"Nil Desperandum." By the Rev. F. Langbridge, M.A.
"Bear and Forbear." By Sarah Pitt.
"Foremost if I Can." By Helen Atteridge.
"Honour is my Guide." By Jeanie Hering (Mrs. Adams-Acton).
"Aim at a Sure End." By Emily Searchfield.
"He Conquers who Endures." By the Author of "May Cunningham's Trial," &c.

Cassell's Picture Story Books. Each containing about Sixty Pages of Pictures and Stories, &c. 6d. each.

Little Talks.
Bright Stars.
Nursery Toys.
Pet's Posy.
Tiny Tales.
Daisy's Story Book.
Dot's Story Book.
A Nest of Stories.
Good-Night Stories.
Chats for Small Chatterers.
Auntie's Stories.
Birdie's Story Book.
Little Chimes.
A Sheaf of Tales.
Dewdrop Stories.

Cassell's Sixpenny Story Books. All Illustrated, and containing Interesting Stories by well-known writers.

The Smuggler's Cave.
Little Lizzie.
Little Bird. Life and Adventures of.
Luke Barnicott.
The Boat Club.
Little Pickles.
The Elchester College Boys.
My First Cruise.
The Little Peacemaker.
The Delft Jug.

Cassell's Shilling Story Books. All Illustrated, and containing Interesting Stories.

Bunty and the Boys.
The Heir of Elmdale.
The Mystery at Shoncliff School.
Claimed at Last, and Roy's Reward.
Thorns and Tangles.
The Cuckoo in the Robin's Nest.
John's Mistake.
The History of Five Little Pitchers.
Diamonds in the Sand.
Surly Bob.
The Giant's Cradle.
Shag and Doll.
Aunt Lucia's Locket.
The Magic Mirror.
The Cost of Revenge.
Clever Frank.
Among the Redskins.
The Ferryman of Brill.
Harry Maxwell.
A Banished Monarch.
Seventeen Cats.

Illustrated Books for the Little Ones. Containing interesting Stories. All Illustrated. 1s. each; cloth gilt, 1s. 6d.

Scrambles and Scrapes.
Tittle Tattle Tales.
Up and Down the Garden.
All Sorts of Adventures.
Our Sunday Stories.
Our Holiday Hours.
Indoors and Out.
Some Farm Friends.
Wandering Ways.
Dumb Friends.
Those Golden Sands.
Little Mothers & their Children.
Our Pretty Pets.
Our Schoolday Hours.
Creatures Tame.
Creatures Wild.

Albums for Children. 3s. 6d. each.

The Album for Home, School, and Play. Containing Stories by Popular Authors. Illustrated.
My Own Album of Animals. With Full-page Illustrations.
Picture Album of All Sorts. With Full-page Illustrations.
The Chit-Chat Album. Illustrated throughout.

Selections from Cassell & Company's Publications.

"Wanted—a King" Series. Illustrated. 5s. 6d. each.
 Great Grandmamma and Elsie. By Georgina M. Synge.
 Robin's Ride. By Miss E. Davenport Adams.
 Wanted—a King; or, How Merle set the Nursery Rhymes to Rights. By Maggie Browne. With Original Designs by Harry Furniss.

The World's Workers. A Series of New and Original Volumes. With Portraits printed on a tint as Frontispiece. 1s. each.

- Dr. Arnold of Rugby. By Rose E. Selfe.
- The Earl of Shaftesbury. By Henry Frith.
- Sarah Robinson, Agnes Weston, and Mrs. Meredith. By E. M. Tomkinson.
- Thomas A. Edison and Samuel F. B. Morse. By Dr. Denslow and J. Marsh Parker.
- Mrs. Somerville and Mary Carpenter. By Phyllis Browne.
- General Gordon. By the Rev. S. A. Swaine.
- Charles Dickens. By his Eldest Daughter.
- Sir Titus Salt and George Moore. By J. Burnley.
- David Livingstone. By Robert Smiles.
- Florence Nightingale, Catherine Marsh, Frances Ridley Havergal, Mrs. Ranyard ("L. N. R."). By Lizzie Alldridge.
- Dr. Guthrie, Father Mathew, Elihu Burritt, George Livesey. By John W. Kirton, LL.D.
- Sir Henry Havelock and Colin Campbell Lord Clyde. By E. C. Phillips.
- Abraham Lincoln. By Ernest Foster.
- George Müller and Andrew Reed. By E. R. Pitman.
- Richard Cobden. By R. Gowing.
- Benjamin Franklin. By E. M. Tomkinson.
- Handel. By Eliza Clarke. [Swaine.
- Turner the Artist. By the Rev. S. A.
- George and Robert Stephenson. By C. L. Matéaux.

⁎⁎ *The above Works (excluding* RICHARD COBDEN*) can also be had Three in One Vol., cloth, gilt edges, 3s.*

Library of Wonders. Illustrated Gift-books for Boys. Paper, 1s.; cloth, 1s. 6d.
- Wonderful Adventures.
- Wonders of Animal Instinct.
- Wonderful Balloon Ascents.
- Wonders of Bodily Strength and Skill.
- Wonderful Escapes.

Cassell's Eighteenpenny Story Books. Illustrated.
- Wee Willie Winkie.
- Ups and Downs of a Donkey's Life.
- Three Wee Ulster Lassies.
- Up the Ladder.
- Dick's Hero; and other Stories.
- The Chip Boy.
- Raggles, Baggles, and the Emperor.
- Roses from Thorns.
- Faith's Father.
- By Land and Sea.
- The Young Berringtons.
- Jeff and Leff.
- Tom Morris's Error.
- Worth more than Gold.
- "Through Flood—Through Fire;" and other Stories.
- The Girl with the Golden Locks.
- Stories of the Olden Time.

Gift Books for Young People. By Popular Authors. With Four Original Illustrations in each. Cloth gilt, 1s. 6d. each.
- The Boy Hunters of Kentucky. By Edward S. Ellis.
- Red Feather: a Tale of the American Frontier. By Edward S. Ellis.
- Seeking a City.
- Rhoda's Reward; or, "If Wishes were Horses."
- Jack Marston's Anchor.
- Frank's Life-Battle; or, The Three Friends.
- Fritters. By Sarah Pitt.
- The Two Hardcastles. By Madeline Bonavia Hunt.
- Major Monk's Motto. By the Rev. F. Langbridge.
- Trixy. By Maggie Symington.
- Rags and Rainbows: A Story of Thanksgiving.
- Uncle William's Charges; or, The Broken Trust.
- Pretty Pink's Purpose; or, The Little Street Merchants.
- Tim Thomson's Trial. By George Weatherly.
- Ursula's Stumbling-Block. By Julia Goddard.
- Ruth's Life-Work. By the Rev. Joseph Johnson.

Cassell's Two-Shilling Story Books. Illustrated.
- Stories of the Tower.
- Mr. Burke's Nieces.
- May Cunningham's Trial.
- The Top of the Ladder: How to Reach it.
- Little Flotsam.
- Madge and Her Friends.
- The Children of the Court.
- A Moonbeam Tangle.
- Maid Marjory.
- Peggy, and other Tales.
- The Four Cats of the Tippertons.
- Marion's Two Homes.
- Little Folks' Sunday Book.
- Two Fourpenny Bits.
- Poor Nelly.
- Tom Heriot.
- Through Peril to Fortune.
- Aunt Tabitha's Waifs.
- In Mischief Again.
- School Girls.

Selections from Cassell & Company's Publications.

Cheap Editions of Popular Volumes for Young People. Bound in cloth, gilt edges, 2s. 6d. each.

- For Queen and King.
- Esther West.
- Three Homes.
- Working to Win.
- Perils Afloat and Brigands Ashore.

The "Deerfoot" Series. By EDWARD S. ELLIS. With Four full-page Illustrations in each Book. Cloth, bevelled boards, 2s. 6d. each.

- The Hunters of the Ozark.
- The Camp in the Mountains.
- The Last War Trail.

The "Log Cabin" Series. By EDWARD S. ELLIS. With Four Full-page Illustrations in each. Crown 8vo, cloth, 2s. 6d. each.

- The Lost Trail.
- Camp-Fire and Wigwam.
- Footprints in the Forest.

The "Great River" Series. By EDWARD S. ELLIS. Illustrated. Crown 8vo, cloth, bevelled boards, 2s. 6d. each.

- Down the Mississippi.
- Lost in the Wilds.
- Up the Tapajos; or, Adventures in Brazil.

The "Boy Pioneer" Series. By EDWARD S. ELLIS. With Four Full-page Illustrations in each Book. Crown 8vo, cloth, 2s. 6d. each.

- Ned in the Woods. A Tale of Early Days in the West.
- Ned on the River. A Tale of Indian River Warfare.
- Ned in the Block House. A Story of Pioneer Life in Kentucky.

The "World in Pictures." Illustrated throughout. 2s. 6d. each.

- A Ramble Round France.
- All the Russias.
- Chats about Germany.
- The Land of the Pyramids (Egypt).
- The Eastern Wonderland (Japan).
- Glimpses of South America.
- Round Africa.
- The Land of Temples (India).
- The Isles of the Pacific.
- Peeps into China.

Half-Crown Story Books.

- Little Hinges.
- Margaret's Enemy.
- Pen's Perplexities.
- Notable Shipwrecks.
- Golden Days.
- Wonders of Common Things.
- Truth will Out.
- Soldier and Patriot (George Washington).
- The Young Man in the Battle of Life. By the Rev. Dr. Landels.
- The True Glory of Woman. By the Rev. Dr. Landels.
- At the South Pole.

Three-and-Sixpenny Library of Standard Tales, &c. All Illustrated and bound in cloth gilt. Crown 8vo. 3s. 6d. each.

- The Half Sisters.
- Peggy Oglivie's Inheritance.
- The Family Honour.
- Krilof and his Fables. By W. R. S. Ralston, M.A.
- Fairy Tales. By Prof. Morley.

Books for the Little Ones.

- Rhymes for the Young Folk. By William Allingham. Beautifully Illustrated. 3s. 6d.
- The Pilgrim's Progress. With Coloured Illustrations. 2s. 6d.
- The History Scrap Book. With nearly 1,000 Engravings. 6s.; cloth, 7s. 6d.
- The Old Fairy Tales. With Original Illustrations. Boards, 1s.; cl., 1s. 6d.
- My Diary. With 12 Coloured Plates and 366 Woodcuts, 1s.
- The Sunday Scrap Book. With One Thousand Scripture Pictures. Boards, 5s.; cloth, 7s. 6d.

Cassell & Company's Complete Catalogue *will be sent post free on application to*

CASSELL & COMPANY, LIMITED, *Ludgate Hill, London.*

www.ingramcontent.com/pod-product-compliance
Ingram Content Group UK Ltd.
Pitfield, Milton Keynes, MK11 3LW, UK
UKHW041227200426
11947UKWH00034B/182